THE NEW TESTAMENT AND MYTHOLOGY

THE
NEW TESTAMENT
AND
Mythology

by

BURTON H. THROCKMORTON, JR.

Philadelphia
THE WESTMINSTER PRESS

PRINTED IN THE UNITED STATES OF AMERICA

To
A. C. T.

Contents

Preface

Perhaps every sensitive man sees his age as a time of crisis. Perhaps he should. In any case, contemporary man knows that from many points of view and for many reasons he lives on a frontier: in a time of rapid change, of the disappearance of many trusted landmarks, of the emergence of many new voices, and of old idols dressed in new, and sometimes intriguing, garb. The Christian, meanwhile, clings to an ancient gospel and proclaims the same Lord. How is he to preach Him in a new age? This book deals with one facet of the highly complex issue of how the church is to communicate the gospel in the modern world. This facet concerns the mythological language and presuppositions of the New Testament kerygma.

I have taken the view of Prof. Rudolf Bultmann as a starting point. Anyone dealing with the subject of the New Testament and mythology must, in one degree or another, take account of and assume a position in relation to the incisive Marburg theologian whose " demythologizing " marks one of the important places in the recent history of hermeneutics. It is Professor Bultmann who has so acutely raised the question of how contemporary man is to understand New Testament mythology; and in doing so he has forced every preacher of the gospel — and, indeed, every Christian believer — to come to terms with, and to some kind of understanding of, the mythological elements of the New Testament. This book, therefore, is written for preachers and for all Christians who are perplexed by (or, at least, interested in) the problem with which it deals. The author does not presume to have settled the issues involved, but he does hope to have shed some light upon them from one perspective.

The summary of Bultmann's principle of hermeneutics, in Part One, is written only for the benefit of the reader who has little or no acquaintance with Bultmann's de-mythologizing. It attempts to present Bultmann's proposal clearly and accurately, and largely in his own words. Here neither defense nor criticism is offered. Chapters IV and V are devoted to a discussion of some of the criticisms that have been registered against Bultmann's interpretation of the crucifixion and resurrection. Chapters VI and VII deal with the crucial question of the nature of mythology. Chapter VIII consists of a brief discussion of eschatology in Bultmann's thought, setting his view against those of a few other contemporary theologians. In Part Three, a re-interpretation of some of the basic issues previously discussed is offered for consideration.

It will be evident to anyone who is familiar with contemporary theological thinking that I am rather inordinately indebted to many teachers and writers. The sources of direct quotation are identified; but many other sources could be named, and how many others there are that I can no longer trace! I should like simply to express my gratitude to the many scholars and teachers and friends who have pointed me to Christ.

There are three men, however, whose names I must record, for reasons I shall refrain from discussing: the late Rev. Charles Franklin Shaw, from whose parish I entered the ministry; Prof. S. Vernon McCasland, who introduced me as an undergraduate to the historical study of the Bible; and Prof. Frederick C. Grant — teacher, scholar, friend — to whom I am especially grateful for many, many things.

Dr. Grant has most graciously read the entire manuscript. He is, of course, in no way responsible for any error of fact or infelicity of interpretation; but his vast knowledge and his sensitivity to the meaning of words and to delicate nuances of thought have greatly improved the whole book. I should like also to thank Dr. Roland W. Tapp, Associate Religious Book Editor, The Westminster Press, for suggesting ways of improving the manuscript. He has been consistently helpful in this, as in many other ways.

I am grateful to Harper & Brothers for permission to quote extensively from Reinhold Niebuhr's essay " The Truth in Myths," in *The Nature of Religious Experience* (1937), ed. by J. Seelye Bixler, Robert L. Calhoun, and H. Richard Niebuhr; to Dean Mervin M. Deems, editor of *The Alumni Bulletin* of Bangor Theological Seminary, for permission to use most of an essay on " The Authority of the Bible " which appeared in Vol. XXIX, No. 4, 1954; and to Herbert Reich, Evangelischer Verlag, and the publisher, Dr. Hans Werner Bartsch, who most kindly allowed me to use innumerable quotations from *Kerygma und Mythos I,* first published in 1948, and soon to appear in a fourth edition.

Finally, but of first importance, I thank my wife, Ansley Coe Throckmorton, for her unfailing support in this, as in every endeavor.

Bangor, 1959   Burton H. Throckmorton, Jr.

PART ONE

Bultmann's Principle of Hermeneutics

CHAPTER I

Introduction

Believers of every historical period must face for themselves the question of how to interpret the message of the
New Testament, for the Bible is not self-explanatory. The
problem of interpretation existed in the early days of the
first preaching; but it has been more acute since the advent of modern scientific thought, and of modern textual,
literary, historical, and form criticism. To be sure, in some
quarters there has been a renewed interest in the Bible,
stemming from the contemporary theological emphasis on
Biblical thought. But this Biblical emphasis has raised
afresh the question of the sense in which the Bible is to be
or can be normative, and has put the theologian in the
position of having to work out some understandable and
acceptable answers to the questions of Biblical authority
and of Biblical interpretation.

The difficulty is not, in the first instance, how to interpret this or that particular text. The problem is more
complex. Before we can determine the meaning of a given
text, we must establish and articulate the point of view
from which we shall read the Bible as a whole. We come
inevitably to any specific text with presuppositions regarding the whole Bible. But one's presuppositions with regard to the Bible cannot be established aside from one's

study of the Bible, that is, aside from one's study of specific texts.

Hence it follows that as one studies the Bible, his presuppositions with regard to it will change. Reading the Bible haphazardly, as one might read bits from a weekly magazine, will not lead to any mature conception of how, from what point of view, one will understand the whole; and when the Bible is so read it cannot be understood in any profound sense. One cannot speak with authority on one verse of Scripture unless one knows something about the whole of Scripture, for it is only in the context of the whole that any single part can be rightly understood and interpreted. And yet it is just the *whole* of the Bible that is so difficult to understand. I suppose anyone, no matter what his presuppositions might be, could find some verses in the Bible with which he most heartily agreed. But should such verses be read in the framework of the Creation, the incarnation, and the *eschaton,* they would tell another story.

The problem that faces the contemporary believer is how to read the Bible as a whole. Biblical texts cannot simply be repeated, parrot-style, and interpreted in their own terms; but the whole Bible must be interpreted in accordance with some principle by which it may be understood. Prof. Rudolf Bultmann has attempted to articulate such a principle. In 1941, Bultmann's " Neues Testament und Mythologie: Das Problem der Entmythologisierung der neutestamentlichen Verkündigung " was first published as part of his volume *Offenbarung und Heilsgeschehen.*

The publication of this volume was undoubtedly one of the most significant events of this generation to have occurred in the field of New Testament hermeneutics. It proposes a new principle of hermeneutics by which the New Testament is to be interpreted in a manner acceptable and understandable to contemporary man; and as the New Testament is pervaded by myths and mythological presuppositions, the proposal is to demythologize the New Testament and at the same time to preserve the kerygma.

Before we turn to an examination of this proposal, a final word of an introductory nature should be said about the meaning of the term " hermeneutics." Hermeneutics is the methodology of interpretation. But before interpretation must come translation. So let us first consider what is involved in translation. Translation is the transference of meaning from one language to another. In the case of the New Testament, because there are so many extant manuscripts, textual criticism must precede translation — theoretically, at least, the best text should be established before translation begins. Unfortunately, however, this is not always possible, as it would be if textual criticism were an exact science, for the establishment of the best text is sometimes partially related to one's prior understanding of the author and of the literature involved. One must apply text-critical methods along with the translating. Translation, however, involves not only a knowledge of the language in which the text being translated is written, and an ability to apply text-critical methods to the thousands of New Testament manuscripts extant; it also involves a prior knowledge and understanding of the work that is being translated. One must translate a writer in accordance with the writer's thought *as one understands it.* It is necessary to emphasize the italicized words, for they indicate the subjective, nonscientific element that enters into all translation.

But to translate is to take only the first step in commu-

nicating an author's message. One must then interpret the
author's meanings in accordance with the author's presuppositions. This is exegesis. Exegesis is the presentation
of what an author meant in accordance with his own presuppositions and with his thought as a whole. It is obvious
that here, even more than in translation, a certain subjective element is unavoidable; for although it is the task
of the exegete to present the author's thought and not his
own, he can do so only *as he understands* the author. However, both translation and exegesis are " scientific " in the
sense and to the degree to which, for example, history is
" scientific." The aim of him who translates and gives the
exegesis is to present accurately the author's thought in the
language of the hearers and in accordance with the author's general point of view.

As has been indicated, however, exegesis is concerned to
interpret meanings. Exegesis is, therefore, also interpretation. The distinction, then, between " Biblical critic "
and " theologian " is a valid distinction only with reference to a difference in emphasis. The Biblical critic must
be a theologian, and the theologian must be a Biblical
critic if they are both to remain relevant. In every historical age the church must relate the kerygma that the New
Testament proclaims to the lives of believers, for each age
is guilty of its own peculiar sins, and each age speaks its
own language; and to each age the judgment and the com-
fort, the hope and the promise, of the gospel must be redefined. The value of the New Testament does not con-
sist primarily in either its history or literature, but in the
fact that, for all who believe, it mediates the Word of
God,[1] that it is the only record of the original response to
God's revelation in Christ of himself and of his will for
men, and that it is the means by which this revelation has

INTRODUCTION 19

been most fully communicated to men. The New Testament is therefore the means whereby a communication is made from God to man; but a communication to man about the meaning and destiny of his life is meaningless to him unless he understands it. It is the purpose of exegesis and interpretation so to interpret the New Testament proclamation as to make it understandable and receivable to contemporary men. How is this interpreting to be done in our generation? It is to this question that Bultmann turns and to which we shall now address ourselves.

II

Professor Bultmann's Proposal

THE PROBLEM

In this and the following chapter we shall briefly outline Bultmann's proposal as it has been reprinted in *Kerygma und Mythos*.[1] Professor Bultmann begins by saying that "the world view of the New Testament is a mythical one."[2] The world is thought of as divided into three stories, with the earth in the middle, the underworld below, and heaven above. God and his angels live in heaven; the underworld is hell, the place of torment. The earth is the place where God and his angels meet with Satan and his demons. Man is not an autonomous being but is constantly subject to the intervening powers of both God and Satan acting directly or through their emissaries. History does not run its course according to laws but is perpetually interrupted by these supernatural powers. This age stands under the power of Satan and is quickly moving toward a cosmic catastrophe which will end it. Then the heavenly Judge will come, the dead will be raised, and all men will be judged — the good to be saved and the evil to be destroyed.

To this mythical world view corresponds a similarly mythical representation of the saving event. (By "saving event " is meant the pre-existence of Jesus, his coming, his life, death, and resurrection, and the emergence of the church.) Bultmann says that the whole event is couched in mythological language: when the time was fulfilled God sent forth his Son. This pre-existent divine Being appeared on earth as a man; his death on the cross on which he suffered as a sinner procured atonement for the sins of men. His resurrection is the beginning of a cosmic catastrophe by means of which death, which was brought into the world by Adam, is destroyed. This raised One has been exalted to the right hand of God in heaven, and he will come again on the clouds of heaven to complete his saving work. Then the dead will be raised, and the judgment will be passed: sin, death, and all suffering will be destroyed. And all this is to occur in the very near future.

All this, continues Bultmann, is mythological language that is derived from the mythology of Jewish apocalyptic and Gnostic redemption myths. " It is for the man of to-day unbelievable, because for him the mythical world picture is a thing of the past." [3] Modern cosmology makes it impossible to derive meaning from such phrases as " He descended into hell " or " He ascended into heaven," for there is undoubtedly no hell beneath and no heaven above. God is not up in heaven; indeed, heaven in the old sense no longer exists for us.

Moreover, the laws of nature have taken the place of spirits and demons. There are for us no demons who are thought to enslave us. Sickness and health have natural causes and are not considered to be the result of the workings of one or another kind of spirit; and the miracles of the New Testament cannot be understood as illustrations of divine intervention. Nor can the mythical eschatology of the New Testament be believed. The end of the world will be a development of nature and not the mythical event of which the New Testament speaks. A man's actions are considered to be the result of his heredity and the history of his experience, and not the result of the entrance of foreign powers into his inner life. " What the New Testament says about ' Spirit ' and about the sacraments is strange and not understandable " [4] to the modern man. Nor can death be understood today as the result of sin; it is rather a necessary event of nature; and inherited original sin is to modern man both " submoral and absurd." [5] So writes Bultmann.

Neither can modern man understand any teaching of substitutionary satisfaction through the death of Christ. How can my guilt be atoned for by the death of a sinless man? What primitive notions of guilt, justice, and of God underlie such an idea? And if this be possible because he who died is the pre-existent Son of God who was afterward raised to the right hand of the Father, in what sense can it be said that he really died? Bultmann completely repudiates any such theory. Finally, from a scientific point of view, the physical resurrection of Christ from the dead is " incredible." All such myths must be eliminated if the kerygma is to be made meaningful.

THE PROPOSAL

The question now becomes, Is it possible to remove the outdated mythology and still preserve the New Testament kerygma? Does the New Testament contain truth that is independent of the mythological language in which the New Testament message has been handed down to us? One cannot answer yes to these questions because he believes he is able to select some parts of the New Testament and reject others. One cannot, for example, reject the legends of the virgin birth and the ascension because Paul and John apparently did not know them. Where would one stop in such a process? And what would be the criterion for this kind of elimination? No, answers Bultmann, one must accept or reject the mythical world picture only as a whole. One cannot simply discard the more obvious " legends " and still hold on to the myths that are more easily rationalized. The same principle must be consistently applied to the whole New Testament.

The preacher owes absolute clarity and preciseness to his hearers. He must tell them what he believes to be true and what he does not believe to be true. Here Bultmann warns the preacher to avoid both muddy thinking and hypocrisy. Is there, then, in the New Testament " nothing but mythology," or does the attempt to understand the real intention of the New Testament lead to the elimination of myth? Bultmann finds an answer already forthcoming from two considerations: (*a*) from the nature of myth and (*b*) from the New Testament itself.

Bultmann declares that the real purpose of myth is not to give an objective world picture, but to illuminate man's understanding of himself in his world. Myths are to be interpreted not cosmologically, but anthropologically — or better, existentially. Bultmann defines myth as it has been defined by the " history of religions " school: the mythological is " that form of representation in which the other-worldly and divine appear as the worldly and human, in which the other side, or transcendent (*Jenseitige*), appears as this side, or immanent (*Diesseitiges*) ." [6] Myths have an existential purpose; they point to truth, not outside of man, but to truth about man. Myth expresses the belief that the origin and purpose of the world in which man lives are not to be found in the world, but that these lie outside the world; myth tells man that " he is not lord of himself, that he is dependent not only upon the world he knows but above all upon outside powers that govern the world he knows "; [7] and finally myth expresses the conviction that man can be delivered from the powers of the world. The process of demythologization has already begun in myth itself, since its purpose is not to paint an objective picture, but to tell man something about himself.

Not only does the purpose of myth, as Bultmann defines it, suggest the possibility of demythologizing, but the New Testament suggests this possibility also in that it contains so many mythological representations, some of which are contradictory. For instance, the death of Christ is represented as both a sacrifice and a cosmic event; and the meaning of the Person of Christ is found in his being both the Messiah and the Second Adam. In addition to the plurality of myths, there are contradictory myths: on the one hand is cosmic determinism, while on the other hand is the call to decision; on the one hand sin is unavoidable, while on the other hand man is responsible. Many words of the New Testament speak directly to the man of today, while many others are meaningless. In this observation Bultmann sees a process of demythologization already begun in the New Testament itself.

Bultmann emphasizes the point that no modern world view can be used as the criterion for demythologizing, for world views change. He does not propose to set a modern scientific world view against an ancient, unscientific one. The criterion must be the understanding of existence that is found in the New Testament itself.

With regard to earlier attempts to demythologize, Bultmann first notes allegorization, which has been used throughout the history of the church. But this "spiritualizing " of events has often led to the elimination of the kerygma.

Bultmann then notes the attempt made by liberal theologians who believed they could solve the problem by elimination — by removing all mythological concepts (the shell) from the New Testament and by recovering the factual, more original, kernel. But of Harnack's attempt Bultmann writes: " The kerygma is here reduced to specific religious and moral principles and to an idealistic ethic religiously motivated. But therewith is *eliminated* the truth of *the kerygma as kerygma,* that is, as the message of the decisive act of God in Christ." [8] These religious and moral ideas were not tied up sufficiently to the historical person through whom they were first called into consciousness.

The New Testament speaks about an event through which God saved men. It preaches Jesus — not primarily his teachings, but his Person as the decisive saving event. Yet it preaches his Person in mythological terms. Can one remove the mythology and still hold on to the Person? That is the question.

Still another attempt to demythologize was made by the " history of religions " school which understood the essence of the New Testament to be, not in its religious and moral ideas, but in its religion — its piety. Although there was truth in this view, the meaning of the New Testament ecclesia was obstructed, and New Testament preaching lost its kerygmatic character, lost sight of the decisive act of God in Christ of which the New Testament speaks. The question is then put: Is it possible to demythologize the New Testament, to reveal the truth of the kerygma as kerygma for men who do not think mythologically?

Bultmann begins the last section of Part One of his work

by saying that he alone cannot complete the task he has undertaken. He can but present the problem, state the principle by the application of which he believes the problem is to be solved, and apply his principle to a few examples. The rest can be done only by a whole generation of theologians.

The New Testament speaks in mythological terms derived from Jewish apocalyptic and Gnostic redemption myths, both of which presuppose a dualism according to which the present world and the men living in it are ruled by demonic powers, and man awaits a salvation that he cannot of himself bring to pass, but that will be accomplished by a redeemer. These myths, says Bultmann, are meaningful, not because of their objective representations, but because of their understanding of human existence; that is, they receive their meaning when they are interpreted existentially. Bultmann then proposes that this is also true of the New Testament — that its meaning will be revealed when it is interpreted existentially, when the question is asked of it, What does this say about my existence, here and now? We must determine whether the New Testament offers man an understanding of his being that will force him to a genuine decision.

Thus Bultmann states the problem. In the New Testament the kerygma is formulated in mythological language, derived primarily from ancient Jewish and Gnostic mythology; and modern man cannot take this mythology seriously because it presupposes an obsolete world view. The solution of this problem in contemporary preaching is not to be found in a selection of certain of the myths and a rejection of others. No criterion exists for making such differentiations. But the New Testament itself points to the way in which it is to be interpreted: it is to be interpreted

existentially. By so interpreting it, the mythological framework can be abolished; and its message — valid for all
time, quite aside from the various world views of different
historical periods — emerges unshackled and understandable. For man remains the same, and the gospel is still good
news for him.

III

Professor Bultmann's Procedure

THE CHRISTIAN UNDERSTANDING OF EXISTENCE

Bultmann analyzes the mythological concepts of world, flesh, sin, anxiety, and death as they are found in the New Testament. Man, believing that he has found his life in visible, tangible realities, boasts in his consciousness of certainty. Actually, the visible realities, those things which are in man's power to dispose of, are all perishing; and he who finds his life in them must perish with them. Man outside of faith knows how precarious this situation is, and so arise on the one hand envy and anger, jealousy and strife, and on the other hand bargains and agreements, and skillful decisions. Out of this grows the anxiety in which each man clings to his own things with the secret feeling that everything — even his life — is slipping away, for the objects of his anxiety are transitory.

In contrast to the life of man outside of faith, Bultmann describes the life that lives out of the invisible and undisposable, that gives up all self-created certainty. This is life " in the Spirit," life in " faith." Such a life is lived in faith in God's grace, in trust that the invisible, unknowable, undisposable meets man as love and opens to him a future that is not death but life.

The grace of God is forgiving grace, freeing man from

28

his sinful past which confines him. All attempts to grasp the visible and disposable are sin because they close the door to the invisible, to the future given by God. To be forgiven for sin is to be freed from one's past; and to be open to the future is to live in faith. Such faith is at the same time obedience, because it is the turning away from oneself, the giving up of all certainty, the renunciation of all attempts to win one's life for oneself, and the entrusting of everything to God who raises the dead (II Cor. 1:9), and who calls into being the things that are not (Rom. 4:17). Such renunciation of everything before God gives one a detachment from all the visible and disposable things of the world, relieves one of anxiety, and gives one an " unworldliness " — gives one freedom.

This " unworldliness," about which Bultmann so often speaks, does not refer to asceticism, but rather to a kind of detachment from the world that, though it encourages participation in the world, discourages ultimate loyalty to the world. One is to live in the world *als ob nicht* ("as if not," I Cor. 7:29-31). The Christian is free from all men but has made himself a slave to all (I Cor. 9:19); the world has been crucified to him, and he to the world (Gal. 6:14). The power of his new life is revealed in weakness, in suffering, and in death (II Cor. 4:7-11; 12:9 f.). It is precisely when he comes to the consciousness of his nothingness that he can be and have everything from God (II Cor. 12:9 f.; 6:8-10).

So to live is to be a " new creation " (II Cor. 5:17). It is eschatological existence. The apocalyptic and Gnostic eschatology has been demythologized in so far as the time of salvation has already broken in for the believer, and the future life has already become present. Bultmann then turns for corroboration to the Johannine literature where

he sees the eschatological myth already demythologized in
the victory that believers now have over the world. Whoever believes already has life and is brought from death
into life (John 5:24 f., etc.). Belief is the victory over the
world (I John 5:14).

But in this eschatological existence the believer has not
a new " nature " (*physis*); he does not arrive at a different
state of existence of which he is certain, the consequence of
which would be libertinism. Nor is he in a new condition
that he must anxiously defend, the consequence of which
would be asceticism. Life in faith is not a condition that
could be described by the indicative; but after the indicative there follows immediately the imperative. The decision of faith is not made once for all, but must be verified
in each new concrete situation so that it is always being
made anew. Freedom does not mean release from the command under which man always stands as man; it means
freedom to obey (Rom. 6:11 ff.). And faith is never fully
grasped but is always in the process of being grasped, ever
wavering between the " not yet " and the " already " (Phil.
3:12-14).

Bultmann then tries to show that Paul himself began to
demythologize the concept of Spirit; and he argues that
from Paul's list of fruits of the Spirit (Gal. 5:22) it is clear
that detachment from the world (which Bultmann believes Paul presupposes) leads to the possibility of a new
openness to one's fellow men.

THE SAVING EVENT

Having portrayed what he believes to be the New Testament understanding of man outside of the Christian
faith, and then having described the life of man in faith,
Bultmann turns to the crucial question of whether the

saving event of Christ can be presented apart from mythological terms. He begins by asking how far it is possible
for the philosopher outside faith and apart from myth to
describe accurately either the predicament of man or the
meaning of salvation. Bultmann has in mind primarily
modern existentialists who in their description of man use
very much the same language that he has used in the fore-
going discussion. But is a Christian understanding of man
possible without Christ? Bultmann states that Heidegger's
analysis of existence appears to be a philosophical analysis
in " secular " language of the New Testament view of human existence.

But is there no difference between the philosophical
statement and the statement of the New Testament? The
author concludes that there is. The philosopher takes human possibility for a fact whereas the New Testament does
not. According to the New Testament, man has lost this
possibility whereas according to the philosopher he has
not. Although philosophy and the New Testament may
describe the state of man in the same terms (as they often
do), the philosopher assumes that either man can alter
his state or that it is unalterable, whereas the New Testament believes that man cannot alter his state but that
Christ can. Philosophy does not realize that man is not
master of his own situation, that man has lost the ability
to be master of his own life because every way he takes in
his fallenness is the way of a fallen man. Outside of Christ,
then, man must despair of the possibility of achieving his
own authentic being. In his self-assertion he is a totally
fallen being, or in theological language, a sinner.

To the question of whether sin is a mythological concept Bultmann answers that at least this much is clear:
" Self-assertion can be understood as guilt only if it can be

understood as ingratitude "; [1] and the necessity of gratitude cannot be known except by one who understands his
life as a gift. Yet this possibility has been lost by man in
his fallenness as is illustrated by pervasive pessimism, by
all talk of the " rights " that life owes, and by all demands
for " happiness," etc. Man, in his radical self-sufficiency, is
blind to his sin, and in this fact is revealed his radical fallenness. Therefore, references to sin *appear* to him as mythological. Here Bultmann denies that the concept of sin is
mythological. He believes he is able to do so because he
has interpreted the concept existentially.

As, then, man is fallen, his real life becomes a possibility
for him only if he is freed from himself, but this he cannot
do of himself. The New Testament, however, says that
where man cannot act, God acts for him — indeed, God
has already so acted. God has freed man from sin, has " justified " him who believes, and does not count men's trespasses against them (II Cor. 5:19). God has made Christ
to be sin for us, that we, in him, might become the righteousness of God (II Cor. 5:21). Everyone who believes
this is acquitted from his past; he is a new creature and
comes as such to every Now; he is free. Thus Bultmann
emphasizes that forgiveness of sins is not meant in the New
Testament in a legal sense as " mere lack of punishment "
in which man's situation would remain essentially the
same; rather, it is truer to say that through forgiveness of
sin man is given freedom from the sin that has imprisoned
him. But this freedom from sin is not to be understood as
a natural quality, but as freedom to obey. Then next to
the indicative stands the imperative. Finally, in so far as
all the commands under which man stands are summed up
in the love command, it is true that man who through
God's forgiveness is freed from himself is at the same time

also freed for self-renunciation on behalf of others (Rom. 13:8-10; Gal. 5:14).

Eschatological existence has thus become a possibility for man, in that God's act in Christ has made an end to the world as " this world " and has made man a " new creation." Here Bultmann quotes from both Paul and John. From the former: " If any one is in Christ, he is a new creation; the old has passed away, behold, the new has come." (II Cor. 5:17.) And from the latter: That the freedom that is given in knowledge of the truth (John 8:32) is freedom from servitude to sin (John 8:34). Jesus calls man out of death into life (John 5:25), out of blindness into sight (John 9:39). The believer is " born again " (John 3:33 ff.), he has received a new beginning; he no longer belongs to the world but he has overcome it (I John 5:4).

Thus the Christ-event is the revelation of the love of God which has freed man " from himself to himself " [2] in that it has freed him to a life of self-renunciation in faith and love. " Faith as a man's freedom from himself, as openness to the future, is only possible as faith in the love of God. . . . Only he who is loved can love, only he who is trusted can trust, only he who has known renunciation can give himself up. We are freed to give ourselves up to God because he has given himself up for us. ' On this is love based, not that we have loved God but that he has loved us and has sent his son as expiation for our sins.' [3] ' We love because he has first loved us.' " [4]

Herein, then, is the difference between philosophy and the New Testament, which distinguishes the Christian from the " natural " understanding of man: " The New Testament speaks and Christian faith knows about an act of God which for the first time makes possible the real life of man in self-renunciation, faith, and love." [5] But is this act of God, about which the New Testament speaks and which Christian faith knows, a myth? And is this freeing of man from himself, to himself, conceivable only as an act of God? Bultmann next turns to these basic questions.

Whoever would assert that any reference to an act of God is mythological would, of course, have to consider as mythological an act of God in Christ. But Bultmann believes that simply to speak of an act of God is not necessarily to speak mythologically. In support of his position he cites the philosopher Wilhelm Kamlah who justifies " mythical language " about a deed of God philosophically.[6] The question is to begin with, Is the Christ-event which the New Testament records a mythical event?

There is no question but that the New Testament records the Christ-event in mythological terms. The question is only whether or not this event *must* be represented mythologically, or whether the New Testament itself leads the way to a demythologized interpretation.

It is clear that the Christ-event is not a myth in the same sense in which the tales of the Hellenistic gods are myths; for although Jesus Christ as Son of God, as a pre-existent, divine being, is a mythical figure, he is also at the same time the historical man, Jesus of Nazareth, who was crucified. History and myth are thus woven together in him: the historical Jesus whose mother and father men knew is at the same time the pre-existent Son of God, and " next to the historical event of the crucifixion stands the nonhistorical resurrection." [7] As a result of this mixture of history and myth, continues Bultmann, certain contradictions stand side by side in the New Testament. Next to the assertion of the pre-existence (Paul, John) stands the legend of the virgin birth (Matthew, Luke) ; next to the ascrip-

tion of humility in human form (Phil., ch. 2) stand the
miraculous proofs in the gospels of divinity, and so on.

But then Bultmann asks what the significance of these
mythological terms is. Is not their intention, he asks, to
express the significance of the saving figure and saving
event of the historical Jesus? If this is the significance of
the mythological language, then one may give up the
mythically objectified forms in which this meaning is conveyed and still preserve the meaning. As an illustration,
Jesus' pre-existence and virgin birth are cited. It is clear,
says Bultmann, that the purpose of these doctrines is not
to give a historical account of Jesus' origin, but to express
the meaning of the Person of Jesus for faith, to one who
believes. And yet, these myths do not augment faith but
rather give the appearance of doing precisely what they
were never intended to do, namely, of contributing to historical knowledge.

It is not for faith, says Bultmann, to question Jesus' historical origin, but to seek his real significance by turning
away from such questions. One is not to question the historical background of Jesus' life and cross, but the meaning of his life is to be found in what God says through it.
Hence Jesus' figure is not to be understood in terms of its
" inner-worldly context," i.e., mythologically. It appears
that for Bultmann mythological language no longer ac-
complishes its original purpose of pointing to the meaning
of the Christ-event for faith; rather does it now point away
from this meaning and is used as historical data.[8] Having
asserted the necessity of eliminating mythological language
as no longer able to contribute to faith, Bultmann turns
his attention to the main questions of the cross and resurrection.

Is the cross, in so far as it is the saving event, to be understood only mythologically; or can it be understood as a historical event, historical not in the sense of its objectifiable, historical context, but in the sense of its meaning as the saving event? The cross is mythically understood when it is described in the objectified representations of the New Testament: the pre-existent, sinless Son of God was crucified; he was the sacrifice whose blood atones for our sin; in his taking sin and death upon himself, he has freed us from death. This mythological language, says Bultmann, is for us not understandable; it also fails to describe the full meaning of the crucifixion. The fact is that much more should be said, namely, that through the cross of Christ the believer is freed from sin as the power that rules over him. " God, who forgave us all our trespasses, blotted out the bond which stood against us with its legal demands, and removed it, nailing it to the cross. He disarmed the principalities and powers and made a mockery of them; in him (Christ) has he triumphed over them " (Col. 2:13-15).

Here the historical event of the cross is exalted to cosmic dimensions. If, then, it is said that the cross is the judgment over the world through which the rulers of this age are destroyed (I Cor. 2:6 ff.), then it is also said that the judgment is passed on us who have fallen victim to the powers of the world. Thus, to believe in the cross of Christ is not to believe in a mythical event that happened outside of us and of our world; it is, rather, to take up the cross of Christ as our own, to be crucified with Christ. As a saving event the cross is not an isolated occurrence in the life of a mythical person, but it is an event that has cosmic meaning. Moreover, it is " the eschatological event; that is, it is not an event of the past to which one looks back, but it is the eschatological event in time and *jenseits der Zeit* (beyond time) " [9] whose meaning in faith is always present, especially in the sacraments. In Baptism, one is baptized into the death of Christ (Rom. 6:3) and crucified with Christ (Rom. 6:6) ; and in the Lord's Supper the death of Christ is continually proclaimed (I Cor. 11:26) . The cross of Christ, then, is present in the daily lives of believers: " Those who belong to Christ Jesus have crucified the flesh with its passions and desires " (Gal. 5:24) . And so Paul speaks further of " the cross of our Lord Jesus Christ, by which the world has been crucified to me, and I to the world " (Gal. 6:14) ; and so also he shares in Christ's sufferings and becomes like him in his death (Phil. 3:10) .

The cross of Christ is a present reality, and not a mythical event. The saving event takes its origin in the historical occurrence of the crucifixion of Jesus of Nazareth. It is the freeing judgment over man. Hence Christ may be said to be crucified " for us " — not in the sense of a mythological theory of sacrifice for sin, but in the sense that one can be crucified with Christ only because Christ himself was crucified. The mythological language is intended to express the meaning of the historical situation. " The preaching of the cross as saving event asks the hearer whether he will appropriate this meaning, whether he will be crucified with Christ." [10]

But does not the cross of Christ receive this meaning by virtue of the fact that it is the cross of *Christ?* Then must a man believe in Christ before he can believe in the saving meaning of his cross? In order to understand the meaning of the cross, must he understand it as the cross of the historical Jesus? Bultmann answers that for the original disciples the answer was yes. They were bound to Christ in a living present, and the crucifixion was an event of their own lives. But for us this relationship is not reproducible, and out of it the meaning of the cross cannot be revealed. For us the cross is an event of the past that cannot be duplicated in our own lives. We know of it as an historical event only through historical reports. But the meaning of the cross is not revealed as a result of a historical inquiry concerning the life of Jesus. Jesus is preached as the crucified One who is also raised from the dead. Cross and resurrection belong together in a unity.

In conclusion, Bultmann discusses the resurrection of Christ. He begins by asking whether the resurrection is not " simply a mythical event." [11] " Can the words about the resurrection of Christ be anything else than the expression of the meaning of the cross? " [12] Does the resurrection say anything else but that the death of Jesus ought not be understood as an ordinary human death, but rather as a freeing judgment of God over the world that destroys the power of death? Does it not simply say that the crucified One did not remain dead but was raised?

Crucifixion and resurrection are indeed, continues Bultmann, one cosmic unity, as Paul seems to imply when he speaks of Jesus as " put to death for our trespasses and raised for our justification " (Rom. 4:25). The resurrection ought not to be viewed as an event subsequent to the crucifixion; but instead, " he who endures death is already the Son of God and his death is itself already the overcoming of the power of death." [13] This is expressed most clearly in the Gospel of John where Jesus' Passion is represented as his glorification and where his being " raised up " has the double meaning of being raised up on the cross and raised up in glory. Here the crucifixion is itself the victory over death; the resurrection and the crucifixion are a cosmic unity in which the world is judged and the possibility of genuine life is created.

If this is so, then the resurrection cannot be understood as a proving miracle that demonstrates the cosmic, eschatological meaning of the cross. Bultmann concedes that in the New Testament the resurrection is so understood. For example, the writer of the book of The Acts says that we know Jesus will judge the world because God has assured us of this " by raising him from the dead " (Acts 17:31); and the Easter stories record proofs that Jesus was raised in bodily form (cf. especially Luke 24:39-43). But these reports are late, and Paul knows nothing about them. Paul, however, on one occasion, does attempt to prove the miracle of the resurrection as a historical event, by citing eyewitnesses (I Cor. 15:3-8). Here Bultmann illustrates the error of Paul's attempt by noting Karl Barth's exegesis which tries to circumvent this difficulty. Barth says that Paul does not cite these witnesses as proof of the historical fact of the resurrection, but rather as proof that he preaches the resurrection just as the earliest church preached it. The witnesses, according to Barth, are meant as witnesses for the Pauline gospel and not for the fact of the resurrection.

Bultmann answers that he can " only understand the text as the attempt to make believable the resurrection of Christ as a historical fact." [14] Here Bultmann finds Paul contradicting himself, for what he says in I Cor. 15:20-22 cannot be stated as a historical fact.[15] However, the resurrection cannot be a proving miracle not only because as a mythical event it is unbelievable, not only because no number of witnesses could guarantee it to one who did not himself believe it, but especially because the resurrection is itself an object of faith and one object of faith (the saving meaning of the cross) cannot be proved by another (the resurrection). The resurrection is an object of faith because it is an eschatological event and as such it cannot be used to prove the eschatological fact of the destruction of the power of death on the cross.

In the New Testament the resurrection of Christ is the eschatological event in which Christ destroyed death and brought life and immortality to light (II Tim. 1:10). Paul uses the idea of Gnostic myths in order to illustrate the meaning of the resurrection; as in Jesus' death all have died (II Cor. 5:14 f.), so also through his resurrection shall all be made alive (I Cor. 15:21 f.). And just as Paul can speak of dying with Christ, so can he also speak of being raised with Christ as a present reality. In the sacrament of Baptism, one not only dies with Christ but one is also raised with him; one not only *will* walk in newness of life, but one *already* walks in newness of life (Rom. 6:4). " You . . . must consider yourselves dead to sin and alive to God in Christ Jesus " (Rom. 6:11). The Christian shares not only in the cross of Jesus but also in his resurrection. To the Corinthians, Paul writes: " We shall live with him by the power of God " (II Cor. 13:4).

The resurrection is, then, not a mythical event that could make the meaning of the cross believable; but the resurrection is believed precisely as the meaning of the cross. " Faith in the resurrection is nothing other than faith in the cross as the saving event, in the cross as the cross of Christ." [16] One does not believe first in Christ and afterward in his cross, says Bultmann, but " to believe in Christ means to believe in the cross as the cross of Christ. It is not the saving event because it is the cross of Christ, but it is the cross of Christ because it is the saving event." [17]

But how does one come to believe that cross to be the saving event if there are no miracles by which to prove it? Bultmann says there is only one answer to this question:

because the cross is preached as such, because the cross is preached with the resurrection. " Christ, who was crucified and raised from the dead, meets us in the proclamation of the Word, and nowhere else. Faith in this Word is the Easter faith." [18] One does not believe this Word as the result of a historical inquiry into its reliability. The proclamation of the Word meets one as God's Word, which is not questioned, but which rather questions the hearer and asks him whether he will believe it or not. Will we believe in the death and resurrection of Christ as the eschatological event that opens to us the possibility of understanding ourselves? This is the question which is asked. To believe is to say yes; to disbelieve is to say no.

The Easter event as the resurrection of Christ is not a historical event; only the Easter faith of the first disciples is historical. The Easter event is an object of faith that is part of the eschatological event. Moreover, " the proclamation of the Word which originated in the Easter event also belongs itself to the eschatological saving event." [19] Through Christ is given the " ministry of reconciliation " and the " message of reconciliation " (II Cor. 5:18 f.) . It is this " message " which leads man to the cross, which makes the cross understandable as the saving event, and which asks man " whether he will understand himself as crucified with Christ and as raised with him." [20] In the preaching of this Word, the crucifixion and the resurrection become present in the " eschatological now." " The eschatological promise of Isa. 49:8 is fulfilled: ' Behold, now is the acceptable time! Behold, now is the day of salvation.' " [21] And in the Fourth Gospel it is written, " Truly, truly, I say to you, he who hears my word and believes him who sent me, has eternal life; and he does not come into judgment, but has passed from death to

life. . . . The hour is coming, and now is, when the dead
will hear the voice of the Son of God, and those who hear
will live" (John 5:24-25). But it is only in the preached
Word that Christ is met: "Faith comes from the proclamation; but the proclamation comes through the Word of
Christ." [22]

Finally, as the Word is part of the eschatological event,
so also is the church in which the Word is preached, and
in which the believers as those who are saved — as those
transferred into eschatological existence — assemble to the
eschatological event. "The word 'church' is an eschatological term; and when it is designated as the 'body of
Christ,' its cosmic meaning is expressed. It is not a historical phenomenon in the sense in which the history of the
world is such; but it is a historical phenomenon in the
sense that it is realized within history." [23]

Bultmann has attempted to demythologize the New Testament proclamation. "Does there remain a mythological
residue?" [24] Whoever thinks that to speak of an act of
God is to speak mythologically will answer yes. But in any
case, it must be granted, says Bultmann, that such mythology is not mythology "in the old sense" — resting upon
mythological world pictures which time has destroyed.
"The saving event of which we speak is not a miraculous,
supernatural event, but a historical event in space and
time." [25] In laying aside the mythological framework in
which the New Testament message is proclaimed, Bultmann believes he has followed the intention of the New
Testament itself in bringing to the fore the paradox of its
message. This paradox is that the one whom God sent is a
concrete historical man, that God's eschatological act was
fulfilled in the fate of this man, and that therefore this
event cannot be proved as eschatological. It is the paradox

that is formulated in terms of him who "emptied himself" (Phil. 2:7), who "though he was rich . . . became poor" (II Cor. 8:9), who though he was God's Son yet was sent "in the likeness of sinful flesh" (Rom. 8:3), who was "manifested in the flesh" (I Tim. 3:16) — the paradox that was classically expressed by John: "The Word became flesh" (John 1:14).

Just as the One in whom God acts in the present, through whom he has reconciled the world to himself, is a real historical man, so is the Word of God not a mysterious oracle but reasonable preaching of the Person and destiny of Jesus of Nazareth, whose historical, saving significance is understandable as a historical phenomenon in relation to a modern world view. But the assertions made of Jesus remain a scandal that is not surmounted in philosophical dialogue but only in obedient faith. Nevertheless, Bultmann maintains that the divine is not made human, as in myth; but the paradox of the presence of the transcendent God in history is still asserted: "The Word became flesh."

PART TWO

Some Criticisms of Bultmann's Proposal

IV

The Crucifixion

CRITICISM BY SCHNIEWIND AND THIELICKE

One of the main objections raised to Bultmann's proposal is that events in the life of Jesus are not considered as events in themselves but as mere " moments " of one's self-consciousness. Thus the danger arises that the kerygma will be separated from its historical roots and not only will thereby be left open to unhistorical, quite arbitrary interpretations, but will, itself, be reduced to a myth. Schniewind asks, " If Bultmann disregards the once-for-all character of Jesus, and understands the Christ-event as related merely to our personal existence, then do not the events of Christ's life become only symbols or (religious) stimuli? " [1] Bultmann is frequently criticized for having disregarded this once-for-all nature of the events of Christ's life, and especially of the crucifixion and the resurrection. Let us first note some of the specific criticisms that have been made of Bultmann's interpretation of the crucifixion.

Schniewind concedes that Bultmann has clarified the " historical meaning " of the cross, but he argues that the historical once-for-allness of the revelation of God is relinquished. The relation of the believer " to the historical cross of Jesus as a past event " is ignored.[2] The result is that " the witness of the New Testament as a whole to the once-for-allness of Jesus " is given up. " While Bultmann emphasizes the event of the cross as a ' historical event,' [3] he does not mean by this an event that happened once on Golgotha. By a historical event he means, rather, the ' eschatological event ' whose meaning is understandable for faith as ' always present.' " [4] Schniewind suggests that instead of referring to Christ as " he in whom God acts in the present," one should speak of him as " he in whom God acts in a once-for-all present." [5]

For Schniewind, then, Bultmann's interpretation of the crucifixion fails to emphasize its character as an event of the *past* that happened once-for-all on Calvary. This situation is the result of Bultmann's existential interpretation which emphasizes the cross's timeless meaning as " always present " in the " eschatological now." And Christianity stands in danger of giving up the very historical roots because of which it supplanted the Hellenistic mystery religions and from which it has always derived its power and authority.

Thielicke criticizes Bultmann from the same point of view. He asks:

Is New Testament history only a vague reality standing behind Christian experience which is scarcely recoverable as it originally occurred? Or is it an event quite distinct from our experience? Is it not the miraculous appearance of the light which shines whether or not the darkness apprehends it? [6]

Thielicke fears that subjective self-analysis becomes normative for Bultmann rather than the gospel, the emphasis being put on the former rather than on the object of faith; and he sees an unfortunate analogy here to Schleiermacher's *Selbstbewusstsein*. He says that in Bultmann's interpretation of the Christ-event there is no reality outside of man's response to it; there is only what takes place in one's consciousness. " The statement in the Johannine Gospel — ' The Word became flesh ' — refers, according to Bultmann, not to a historical fact which took place in a stable in Bethlehem, but to the changing of my self-understanding which is derived from that historical incident." [7] In short, Thielicke charges Bultmann with making the historical report of the New Testament not an event in itself, but only a prologue to an event — namely, the event of my changing self-consciousness; and he adds that the " historical events " of which Bultmann speaks are events that concern only one's " existential self-understanding." [8] Bultmann emphasizes the relation of the Christ-event to one's experience, rather than the historical fact itself, by referring to its occurrence in the " eschatological now."

Schniewind suggests that the event does not recur, that it happened only once and can never happen again, but that it is remembered. The Christ-event " is an event in a causally related series of events, an event in human history, which is passed on through remembrance, and is investigated in historical research." [9] Bultmann, however, makes a distinction that Schniewind denies. Bultmann states that the events of the first century which are reproduced only in memory cannot be the saving events; for past events which are present in the memory cannot be present in " existence." [10] For Bultmann, the saving event is present in " existence " and not simply in memory. Schniewind affirms, however, that the distinction between what is known in remembrance and what is known in existence is false; that there is no genuine antithesis between memory and existence, for the former is essential to the latter.[11]

Bultmann's Answer

What is Bultmann's answer to these criticisms which are basically one: that in his proposal the Christ-event loses its historical once-for-all character as an event to be investigated by historical inquiry, and is made repeatable in human experience when in fact it is only to be remembered? Bultmann replies that he does not deny the historical nature of the cross. He writes:

> Were I to ignore the relation of faith to the historical cross of Jesus as a past event, I would give up, it is granted, the confession and kerygma of the New Testament. But that is not at all my intention. I am concerned with the historical significance of the once-for-all historical event which, despite its once-for-all historical character, is *nevertheless* the eschatological event. . . . The once-for-all event of the past is constantly present.[12]

By this, Bultmann does not mean the " timeless presence of an idea ";[13] this, he acknowledges, would reduce the cross to a symbol. He thus denies Schniewind's accusation that in his proposal the events of Christ's life become only symbols. And indeed I believe that Bultmann is at least partly correct in his defense of his position. The events in Christ's life are for Bultmann real, past events and not merely symbols of events or eternal ideas. For Bultmann, one can be crucified with Christ — his existential interpretation of the significance of the crucifixion — only because Christ himself has already, at a point in past time, been crucified. Jesus' crucifixion cannot be mythological for Bultmann, precisely because it is historical. The crucifixion, together with Jesus' life and teachings, are also for Bultmann subjects for historical inquiry — as, for instance, his book *Jesus and the Word* shows;[14] but histori-

cal inquiry cannot reveal the meanings of the events. Yet
it must be emphasized that Bultmann considers the crucifixion as a historical event that took place at a definite
point in time and was witnessed by many. He writes:

> As saving event the cross of Christ is not a mythical
> event, but a historical fact which originated in the his-
> torical event of the crucifixion of Jesus of Nazareth.[15]

And again, the disciples " witnessed the cross of him with
whom they had lived in a personal relationship." The cross
" was for them an event of their own lives." [16] I cannot
agree with those who accuse Bultmann of failing to recognize the historical nature of the cross. This, as he says, was
not his intention; nor, I believe, may he be justly so
charged.

But must the cross lose its once-for-all character when it
is said to be " made present " in the preaching? Schniewind insists that a past event can never be made present,
but is only remembered. Bultmann answers that the revelation is more than " the mere report of a past fact." [17] In
this connection he considers Schniewind's " speaking of a
unique and final revelation of God in history " as danger-
ous, because it is apt to make of the revelation a " reve-
latum, something which happened in the past and is now
an object of detached observation," and because it ob-
scures an understanding of the revelation as always present in the church.[18] One must not forget, he says, that
" now is the day of salvation." When merely a historical
fact of the past, the cross is not an event of our own lives,
as it was in the lives of the first disciples; it is a historical
event that preceded the time of our experience. But the
cross is met in the preaching and is thereby made present.[19] Bultmann denies that he has attacked the once-for-

allness of Jesus from which, he agrees, the preaching takes its origin and its legitimacy. But it is the paradox of this event which happened once-for-all that it is made present in the preaching. This is so because both the cross and the preaching are eschatological events.

Bultmann thus disagrees with Schniewind's interpretation of the cross as " remembered," and he makes a distinction between the remembrance of events in one's own past and the remembrance of events that the historian reports. This is, I think, a legitimate and necessary distinction. Bultmann writes:

> It is correct to say that remembrance is an intrinsic element of human existence, yet only in so far as I remember *my* past. . . . But the remembrance which the historian creates when he reproduces facts of the past is something quite different, which can plainly endanger or destroy historical existence. Indeed, the historian confronts the past, but not in so far as he reproduces events of the past but only in so far as he meets human existence and its meaning in the past (as his history). The " remembrance " of the kerygma is something else. This presents neither facts of the past as they are discovered, nor does it lead to a confrontation of human existence and its meaning, but — as a sacramental event — it (the remembrance of the kerygma) re-presents the past event so that the same event is renewed for me to confront it.[20]

" Remembrance " of the Crucifixion

Bultmann is saying, in effect, that there is a significant difference between the Christ-event and all other historical events. A man remembers an experience in his own life in a way quite different from his remembrance of any other past historical events. His first day in school (if it is remembered) or his wedding day (if he is married) is not remembered at all in the same way in which, for instance, Balboa's discovery of the Pacific Ocean is remembered. The reason is that what I have seen myself I can know (and therefore remember) in a way in which I can never know (and therefore remember) what someone else has seen and reported, and about which I may only read. Such a report is always subject to investigation and verification.

Moreover, if it is the report of a meaningful event — and that is the only kind of event in which a person is interested — its meaning, as someone else has understood it, is incorporated into the report of the event; and the historian thus becomes involved in the highly subjective task of divorcing interpretation from fact and of reinterpreting in the interest of accuracy. The meaning, then, of a historical event can never be arrived at directly — through immediate experience — but is always derived indirectly through the report of one witness (in which case the meaning may be highly questionable) or of more witnesses (in which case the meaning may be increasingly confused as the number of reports is increased). Therefore, the meanings of events I remember through historical reports about them can never be as certain, as decisive, or as personal — *for me* — as are the meanings of events in which I have myself participated. Reports must always remain subject to question in the light of other reports, and they must always remain merely *reports,* referring to nonexperienced events.

Now let us return to the matter of Jesus' crucifixion. Do I know about this event only as a historical fact which I remember in the same way in which I remember any other historical data? If I do, then I know of the cross only through historical inquiry, and my certainty of the event is dependent upon the authenticity of the reports which

other data not yet investigated or discovered might contradict — the final decision being, in any case, not with me
but with the historian. My faith in the reality of the event
would remain subject to another's verification.

Moreover, granted that the historians concede the occurrence of the event, if it is solely a historical event, the
meanings to be ascribed to it or derived from it are also
to be determined by others than myself. If I experience
an event myself, I arrive at its meanings firsthand — or, at
least, at the meaning it has for me; and this meaning remains authentic and decisive for me. But the meaning of
a historical event is already attributed to it before I know
about it, and it is for the historian (and not for me) to
validate, to invalidate, or to reinterpret such meanings. I
should be obliged to accept the conclusions of historians
with regard to the legitimacy of the interpretations that
the New Testament authors gave to the historical event
of the crucifixion. Then, if the cross is solely a historical
event, both the reality of the event and the meaning of the
event are for the historian to decide, which is not the case
with an event in which I have myself participated.

But if God's revelation of himself in Christ has been recorded in the New Testament, and if the New Testament
is the medium by which this revelation is communicated
to me, then I must confront the New Testament personally, or I cannot receive the revelation, for it is the nature
of revelation to be known only directly. So I must meet
the event of the cross and the interpretations that the New
Testament gives it directly, and not by way of a historian,
if the New Testament is to be revelatory to me.

The event, then, if it is revelation, *must* be known directly and is therefore removed from the realm in which
the historian's word is decisive. This is not to say that his-

torical study will not enlarge my understanding of the
interpretations of the event; it is only to say that such
study need not discredit or eliminate them. This is so because I do not remember the crucifixion as I remember
other historical events, but I remember it as an event that
I have personally confronted and experienced. Moreover,
paradoxically, I have confronted this event through the
eyes of interpreters, so that the interpretation is inseparable from the event. In other words, I have confronted
the event, interpreted; I know it to be true because I have
experienced it, but I have experienced it with its meanings already given.

To the believer, the cross minus New Testament interpretations is an irrelevant abstraction. And so it is that
the events through which God revealed himself in Christ
are unique in that they are interpreted historical events
that are also experienced by the believer. In the case of
these events through which God revealed himself in Christ,
they are both historical and experienced by the believer;
and yet their meaning, being inextricably bound up with
the record about them, is to be determined neither by the
historian nor by him who experiences them, for the events
are experienced as already interpreted.

This is not to say, of course, that the believer does not
interpret the meanings that the events recorded in the
New Testament have for him; for every believer in every
age must do this. But the believer does not interpret an
uninterpreted event; he interprets for himself an event to
which a more primary significance has already been attributed. In other words, the believer interprets an event
already interpreted, and his interpretation is therefore
always secondary and derived.

I agree with Bultmann, therefore, that the cross is confronted in the preached Word and is not remembered in the same way as are other historical events. But I disagree with him when he limits the meaning that is given in this confrontation to a single New Testament interpretation — an existential one. For Bultmann, when one confronts the cross its meaning is understood only in terms of dying with Christ and of being raised with him; whereas in the New Testament the crucifixion is preached with more than one meaning. But in Bultmann's demythologization only one existential meaning is left to him, and nothing can be said about any other New Testament interpretation which Bultmann cannot demythologize.

In Part Three we shall discuss this limitation which pervades Bultmann's whole proposal, and we shall suggest existential meanings which are to be found in the New Testament interpretations of the cross but which Bultmann has rejected as incapable of demythologization.

V

The Resurrection

BULTMANN'S INTERPRETATION

Let us state briefly Bultmann's interpretation of the resurrection before we note the points at which it has been criticized.[1] For Bultmann, to speak of the resurrection is to speak of the meaning of the cross, which is to understand the death of Christ as the freeing judgment of God over the world wherein death was conquered. Cross and resurrection are one cosmic event, and Jesus' death is *in itself* the overcoming of the power of death. Moreover, the resurrection cannot be understood as a miracle that proves the meaning of the crucifixion even though it is so understood in the New Testament when it speaks of the empty tomb and the bodily appearances. The resurrection cannot be a proving miracle because (*a*) it is unbelievable, (*b*) witnesses cannot prove it, and most important (*c*) because it is itself an object of faith and one object of faith cannot prove another.

The resurrection is an object of faith because it is an eschatological event; hence it cannot be a proving miracle. And the resurrection is an eschatological event because the New Testament affirms not only that one dies with Christ but also that one is raised with him in the present. The Christian not only *will be* but *is* a new creation. The resurrection faith is, then, faith in the cross as saving event; and the cross is the saving event not because it is the cross of Christ; rather is it the cross of Christ because it is the saving event. If the latter is true — if it is not because it is *Christ's* cross that one believes it is the saving event — how does one come to believe it as such?

One believes the cross to be the saving event because it is preached to him as such: the cross is preached with the resurrection, or the cross is preached as the saving event. The Easter event is not historical as the resurrection of Christ; it is historical as the beginning of the belief in the resurrection — as belief in the cross as the saving event. If, then, one knows the cross to be the saving event because it is so preached to him, the Word of the preaching also belongs to the eschatological event, as does the church in which this Word is preached.

THIELICKE'S CRITICISM

Now let us note some of the major criticisms that have been brought against this interpretation. Thielicke criticizes Bultmann in saying that for Bultmann "the resurrection is the result of a meeting understood metaphorically and is in no sense at all an event." [2] He insists that faith in the resurrection must be more than a "reflex of an experienced encounter" and must be "grounded in history." [3] Both of these criticisms are slightly confusing because, in the first place, Bultmann does not interpret the resurrection as "the result of a meeting understood metaphorically" but as the result of an encounter with the cross of Christ; and, in the second place, Bultmann does not understand faith in the resurrection as a "reflex" (by which word Thielicke wishes to indicate the "relativity of psychologism" [4]) but as a genuine response of the whole person to the crucifixion. To be sure, however, Bultmann does not understand Jesus' resurrection as an "event"; and with this point we shall deal in Part Three. But Thielicke maintains that the New Testament reports it as a historical event, and as such it must be proclaimed.

CRITICISM BY SCHNIEWIND AND OTHERS

Schniewind maintains that once-for-allness is as essential a characteristic of the resurrection as it is of the crucifixion; but when the resurrection is interpreted as the meaning of the cross it loses this character. The resurrection, he insists, must be viewed as a once-for-all event. "The testimony declares that Jesus the crucified lives and reigns — that the crucified One is also the One who was raised. It declares the once-for-allness of what God did in Jesus of Nazareth." [5] Schniewind also maintains that "what meets us in the kerygma of the church is not the Easter faith but the Easter witness of the first disciples. The faith says nothing about itself." [6] Bultmann agrees that this is true in the New Testament; but he adds that he "cannot acknowledge" such lists of witnesses "as kerygma" but sees them only as "fatal, because they furnish proof for the authenticity of the kerygma." [7] But Schniewind strongly objects to Bultmann's terming such arguments "fatal" because he finds them so commonly used in the early preaching.[8] He argues that the New Testament witness is to the resurrection as a historical event that is frequently confirmed as such.

Others insist on maintaining the historical authenticity of the stories of the empty tomb as well as of the bodily appearances. Paul Althaus has asserted that with the first disciples the fact of the empty tomb belonged together with the resurrection appearances, and that the belief in the resurrection rested from the beginning on both of these bases.[9] He also emphasizes that the appearances were not " visionary " but " bodily." [10] In another pointed attack on Bultmann's whole point of view, H. Sasse has insisted on the necessity of believing in the resurrection as it has been reported to us — namely, as a historical event.[11] Moreover, Markus Barth has tried to show, in opposition to Bultmann, that the seeing and the touching of the body of Jesus after it was raised from the dead must be considered as historically unquestionable.[12]

KÜMMEL'S CRITICISM

In an exceedingly interesting article, W. G. Kümmel has maintained that to give up the resurrection as a historical event is also to forfeit the kerygma. He writes, " If one gives up the New Testament belief in the resurrection as an *event* in history, one gives up the reality, for believers, of the resurrection of the crucified One and with it the reality of the *historical,* saving act of God." [13] And so, also, is given up the beginning of the Lordship of Christ,[14] and the beginning of the " end-time " community of Christ measured from the point in time of the event of his resurrection. And so the future expectation of the New Testament loses its real meaning.[15] " On this point, then, there can be no doubt that the demythologizing of the New Testament is not possible without giving up the New Testament kerygma which must be expressed here in mythological language." [16] Although one cannot demythologize major New Testament doctrines, such as the resurrection and the final, eschatological events which can only be expressed in mythological language, Kümmel proposes that " border statements " which may not be essential to the New Testament (such as those concerning the empty tomb and the thousand-year reign of Christ) be carefully examined. This kind of criticism of myths in the New Testament he deems necessary.[17]

KARL BARTH'S CRITICISM

Let us look, finally, at Karl Barth's defense of orthodoxy against Bultmann.[18] Barth analyzes Bultmann's understanding of the resurrection as follows: According to Bultmann, at the resurrection " he, Jesus himself, exists in this history and time only in the belief of the disciples. The self-manifestation of the raised One is realized in the disciples and *only* in them. *Nothing* happened between him and them. There was no new, decisive, basic meeting between him and them from which their belief arose. Only *they* were in this time; he was *not*. They were alone. . . . The deed of God was identical with their belief. That they believed was the real content of the Easter faith." [19] Barth then criticizes Bultmann's interpretation at five points:

He asks, " Is it true that one can affirm as true a theological statement only when he can prove it to be an integral part of the Christian understanding of human existence? " He answers, " No." Theological statements, he says, " are not to be reduced to statements about the inner life of man." [20] One must agree wholeheartedly.

Barth asks, " Is it true that, in the face of a historical event in time, one can acknowledge it as a true occurrence only if one is in a position to prove it as a historical fact " — by the methods of the " still silent " presuppositions of modern historical criticism? He believes this is Bultmann's meaning, and answers, " No," adding that " the whole Bible contains very little ' history.' " [21] But this is not quite Bultmann's point. Bultmann wishes to make a distinction between " true occurrences " expressed as " historical fact " and " true occurrences " expressed mythologically. He does not demand historical verifiability as Barth's criticism implies, but demythologization (or existential interpretation) of the truth expressed mythologically.

Barth argues that even in the New Testament the message has the character of " strangeness," and that it was as unbelievable to the first disciples as it was to the educated on the Areopagus.[22] This criticism seems to be based on the assumption that Bultmann's criterion for elimination is always " strangeness " or " unbelievableness." But this is not so. Bultmann eliminates what is mythological, but not what is " strange " or " unbelievable " *because* it is such. Indeed, Bultmann's interpretation of the meaning of the cross *is* " strange " and " unbelievable " except in faith; and he writes that the *skandalon* of the kerygma will " not be overcome in philosophical discussions, but only in obedient faith." [23] Bultmann's purpose is not to eliminate the *skandalon* of the gospel, but to identify it correctly. He sees modern man wrongly identifying the strangeness of the gospel as consisting in its first-century cosmology.

Barth says that contemporary thought on the subject of world views is neither so closed nor such a unity as one would be made to believe " under the dictatorship of the Marburg-Kant school." [24] This is no doubt a criticism that is legitimate when applied to many areas of Bultmann's theology, and especially in connection with his understanding of eschatology. It is to be agreed that Bultmann tends to presuppose the universality of his own kind of rationalism.[25]

Finally, Barth asks, " Is it not catastrophic when Bultmann requires us to accept the mythical world view (of

the first century) either as a whole or not at all, as if
Christianity were commanded to accept or reject world
views?" [26] Of course, Christianity is not required to make
final judgments on world views; but the believer inevitably assumes *some* world view, held either explicitly or
implicitly. And if the kerygma is to be preached meaningfully, it must be articulated in terms of an understandable
world view. Bultmann is arguing for the elimination of a
mythical world view because such a world view becomes
in our day the *skandal* of the gospel when, in fact, the
skandal of the gospel has nothing to do with world views.

With four matters raised in this chapter, I shall deal
later: (*a*) with Kümmel's objection that in Bultmann's
understanding of the resurrection the future expectation
loses its real meaning, I shall deal in Chapter VIII, on
" Eschatology "; (*b*) in Chapter VI, on " Mythology," I
shall discuss Kümmel's proposal that " border statements "
be carefully examined but that basic doctrines be left un-
touched; (*c*) with the view commonly expressed, but most
clearly by Karl Barth, that according to Bultmann there
was no new, decisive meeting between Christ and his disciples — no once-for-all event — from which the disciples'
belief arose, and (*d*) with Barth's implicit denial that a
theological statement may be true even when it does not
make an affirmation about the Christian understanding of
human existence, I shall deal in connection with my own
proposal in Part Three on which they have either a positive or negative bearing. There are, however, two major
objections that have been frequently raised against Bultmann's interpretation of the resurrection with which I
cannot agree and which I should like at this point to
discuss.

Bultmann's interpretation stems from his understanding of the difference between history and revelation, and history and myth, and from his concept of myth. In so far as this interpretation is derived from his analysis of the difference between history on the one hand, and revelation and myth on the other, I am in agreement with it. It is due to the narrow limits he sets for the nature and function of myth that his interpretation of the resurrection becomes inadequate. The two objections to Bultmann's interpretation of the resurrection to which we have referred are derived not from his understanding of myth, but from the distinction he makes between history and revelation, and history and myth. The objections are: (a) that Bultmann does not regard the resurrection as a historical event, and (b) that he does not consider Jesus' bodily resurrection appearances or the empty tomb to be either historical facts or proofs of the resurrection. They are for him mythological. In these two respects I consider Bultmann to have made a contribution toward clarifying the current ambiguity which too simply identifies both revelation and myth with history.

The Resurrection Not a Historical Event

Let us now consider the distinction to be made between history and revelation. The noun " history " denotes either an account of past events, or it denotes those events which are recorded in an account. Similarly, the adjective " historical " may be used to describe any event which one has reason to believe actually took place, or any account of events which one has reason to believe is accurate or relatively accurate. But the terms " history " and " historical " are ambiguous, as they can be used in two quite different senses. On the one hand, it may be said of an event, " It is history " — meaning that it happened, that the fact that it

happened is verifiable or at least reasonably to be supposed, and that anyone who had been there when it happened could have witnessed it. But, on the other hand, the
word " history " is also used to denote not primarily an
event itself, but a particular account of an event. According to this meaning of the word " history," when one says,
" It is history," he means that it is to be read in an account
of past events. And so we speak of " history books " and of
" histories," meaning that what is to be read in such books
is an account of past events — of history as it was described
in the first definition.

Now, at first glance, there may not appear to be any dis-
crepancy between these two uses of the word " history ";
for one would suppose that what is recorded in an account
of past events is precisely what happened. But when the
word " history " is used in the latter sense a significant ambiguity sets in, for all recorded history is of necessity interpreted history. The very fact that it was recorded is in
itself an interpretation of its significance in the judgment
of a particular historian in that it was worth recording. It
was, however, worth recording *from a particular point of
view*, and may not have been worth recording from another point of view. And every time an event is rerecorded
its significance is re-established.

But not only is an event to be considered as interpreted
simply by virtue of the fact that it is recorded; it is further
interpreted by what the author says or does not say about
it — by the latter as much as by the former. Every historian must reinterpret his sources which are themselves
interpreted when he meets them; and so it is that history
can never " entirely dispense with the fictional element." [27]
Nor is there any absolute criterion by which a historian is
enabled to judge on the accuracy of the interpretations

that he has received in his sources. He cannot rely on the oldest sources as necessarily being the most accurate because they are the oldest, for often a firsthand witness of an event is too close to it to see it in a wider and therefore truer perspective. And so the process develops — an event is interpreted; then it is reinterpreted; then there are two accounts for a third historian to reinterpret, and so on for as long as men record history.

Nor is it true that the less historical events are interpreted the better the accounts of them are. For a man reads history not in order to cast his eyes over a multiplicity of meaningless, unrelated facts of the past, but in order to fit the past together into some kind of coherent, intelligible pattern which in turn helps him to understand not simply his past for its own sake, but also his present and, in many cases, what some of the possibilities for the future are. The good historian will, therefore, not simply set down a list of past occurrences in chronological order; [28] but he will further interpret the significance of the events he has recorded in accordance with his own particular world view. Hence, the good historian will not consider only the accuracy of his sources and the faithfulness with which he transcribes them; he must also accept or reject, in whole or in part, the interpretations that his sources inevitably contain, and he must seriously consider the world view in accordance with which he will himself reinterpret. A historian's world view, his philosophy of history, his understanding of human existence, and his faith about the beginning and the end, are the decisive factors in his account of the history that he records. The great historian is not the man who most accurately transcribes the minutiae of which he alone has knowledge; rather is he the man who most profoundly understands the meaning of the historical data he has assembled, who can clarify major issues and relate them to the details that he has patiently sought out and whose proper relevance in the total scheme he rightly understands.

It becomes clear that uninterpreted history is a meaningless abstraction, for all history involves interpretation and no event is recorded simply as an event in itself but only because it is considered to have significance, no matter how minute. Even a simple historical record of a name and a date of birth presupposes a judgment made by the recorder that the memory of these two facts was worthy of being perpetuated. And so one man's opinion contributes to historical data, but only because it was in the first instance related to a meaningful fact.

But it is also clear that there are degrees of interpretation, and that there are of necessity conflicts in interpretation. An event that is meaningful to one historian because it illustrates for him a time of economic prosperity enjoyed by a nation under study may be significant to another historian as revealing the moral decadence of the given nation. Hence, histories are rewritten over and over again, partly to incorporate newly discovered data, but partly also to reinterpret the significance of the same data.

Now let us consider the relation of revelation to history. Revelation, as the Bible understands it, involves a particular interpretation of historical events. Any event that a witness understands as an event in which God acted is for that witness revelation. Revelation, then, is given in and through historical events, but it is not understood as revelation except by one who sees the hand of God in such events. It is quite possible, therefore, as it is indeed the case, that the same historical event will be revelatory to one witness and not to another. The revelation is not visible as revelation except to one who will accept it as such; to all others it is an event that must either be interpreted in another way or that has not been visible at all. Because revelation is an interpretation of an event as an act in which God was at work, it is believable only in faith.

Revelation can never be demonstrated to be revelation because it can never be proved that what one man has interpreted as an act of God or as an event in which God has acted was actually such. The event in which God has acted may be demonstrable; the interpretation of the event as one in which God spoke to a believer is not. Hence revelation is given in history, but it is not the same as history; and any event *may* be revelatory.[29] Revelation is historical occurrence interpreted, and interpreted from a particular point of view. Revelation is historical from one point of view but it is not historical from another. It is historical in that it is given in history and is understood as historical by those who receive it as revelation, but it is not historical in that it is not visible to an individual who will not or cannot receive it as a manifestation of the Divine. The event through which the revelation is given may or may not be seen; but the revelation that is given through the event is not visible and so cannot be understood as history by those who either cannot see it or who reject it as revelation.

The concept of revelation, therefore, includes two points of reference, or two poles, that stand in a polar unity with each other: (*a*) it includes a reference to a historical occurrence; and (*b*) it includes a reference to an interpretation of that occurrence as an event in which God acted. In the following discussion the term " history " will be used to describe only the first reference; and the term " revelation " will include both of the two poles in a unity.

We shall distinguish between history and revelation, meaning by history an occurrence that is visible to all, and by revelation an occurrence in which faith sees the hand of God.[30]

Both the Old and New Testaments, which record God's continuing revelation to men culminating in Jesus Christ, bear out this distinction between history and revelation. Israel's social injustice in the eighth century B.C. is history; but it was Amos who, observing a historical situation viewable by all his countrymen, saw in that situation that God was just and would mete out justice. God *revealed* himself to Amos, in historical circumstances and events, as a God of justice. The history — the social injustice — was verifiable; the revelation that God is just was not.

Indeed, the revelation given to the prophets was not only undemonstrable; it was *rejected* by many — often, perhaps, by most — of the people who stood with them in the *same* historical situations. Many witnessed the same event or events, but the revelation was given to one. Whereas others only saw, the prophets also heard; whereas others only heard, the prophets also saw. The masses saw only what was demonstrable; but the prophets also saw what they could not prove even to those who stood beside them and participated with them in the same events. And what the prophets saw — what they recorded as revelation — was of far greater significance both for their own day and for succeeding generations than what the masses saw and reported as history, as verifiable events.

Now let us consider Jesus' resurrection. Was it history? By this is meant, Was it visible for anyone present to witness? Or was it revelation? By this is meant, Was it an interpretation of a historical event that was receivable only by faith? I think the New Testament forces us to conclude that it was the latter. Jesus was not seen by the masses who see historical events, by " all the people " (Acts 10:41), but only by those who had known him in the flesh, who had taken part in the preceding historical events of his life and crucifixion, and who had been " chosen by God as witnesses " (Acts 10:41). The disciples saw what those in whose midst they stood did not see; and it was given to them, as it had been given to the prophets before them, to preach to their contemporaries what had been revealed.

If Jesus had been raised in a physical body, his resurrection would have been a historical event to be demonstrated simply by pointing to him; and Jesus would have been seen by multitudes in Galilee and Jerusalem, and presumably on the road in between by men and women who had never been his disciples. All would have believed, for his resurrection would have been revealed to all. No; his resurrection would have been *revealed* to no one, for it would have been a historical event.[31] If Jesus' resurrection had been a historical event, none could have doubted; but if his resurrection had been a historical event, none could have *believed*, for it would have been *revealed* to none, and would have been *known* by all. It would have been an event to be recorded as verifiable history, rather than an event to be preached as revelation; but it was the latter. It was the event in which God revealed, to eyes that could see, the significance of the crucifixion and the ultimate meaning of life. What I can see and hear and touch, I know, I do not believe; but I desire to believe more than to know.

The fact of the resurrection, known only in faith by those to whom it was revealed, was not, then, demonstrable. It was an interpretation of an event that took place in the lives of those who had been closely related to

Jesus' historical life. Christ, raised, was known only by revelation. But the disciples wanted to prove to an unbelieving world what they could not prove, and thus they began to historify what was not really demonstrable history. They gradually removed the resurrection from the realm of faith and revelation to the realm of knowledge and provable history. One can see this development quite clearly in the New Testament.

It is generally conceded among historical scholars that the earliest known account of the resurrection is in I Cor., ch. 15. In this account Paul does not report Jesus' appearances as physical in nature. The only word Paul uses for "appear" is ōphthē — the same word that is used in Luke to describe the appearances to Jesus of an angel while he was praying on the Mount of Olives before his crucifixion. Paul also used another form of the same word in I Cor. 9:1 where he exclaims, "Have I not *seen* Jesus our Lord?" as well as in Rom. 15:21 where he quotes the Septuagint exactly (except for the order of one word) and where the meaning is clearly to "know" or "understand." The only other place in which we may be sure Paul used the word is in I Thess. 5:15 where it is used idiomatically in the expression "*see* to it" — that is, make certain.[32] Horaō was not the word commonly used to express literal seeing, this meaning being more frequently expressed by the verbs blepō and theōreō. Horaō was more usually used to describe appearances of divinity, or appearances in dreams, or to describe perceiving, or discerning, or experiencing.[33] In I Cor., ch. 15, however, Paul undoubtedly does not use ōphthē to describe literal seeing with the eyes, for he uses the same word to describe Jesus' appearance to himself and his appearances to the disciples perhaps five years earlier.[34] One may not presume to believe that Paul thought Jesus' physical body remained on the earth for possibly as long as five years after the crucifixion.

Moreover, Paul apparently knew no doctrine of the ascension that could have accounted for the fact that Jesus could not still be seen in the flesh in the years of Paul's preaching. " In the earliest tradition," writes Professor Grant, ". . . the resurrection and the ascension were probably viewed as one event." [35]

Paul also insists that " flesh and blood cannot inherit the kingdom of God " (I Cor. 15:50) — a statement that is difficult to reconcile with a belief in Jesus' physical resurrection, since Paul bases his belief in the resurrection of believers on his faith in the resurrection of Christ. Kirsopp Lake has written:

> According to the Pauline epistles the resurrection of Christians will be a change from a *sōma psychikon* to a *sōma pneumatikon*, for flesh and blood cannot inherit the Kingdom of God (I Cor. 15:44 and 50). Inasmuch as Paul bases this anticipation of the resurrection or metamorphosis of Christians on the model of the resurrection of Jesus, who was the first fruits (I Cor. 15:23), he must have held that the risen Lord had a "spiritual" body, or, in other words, was a Spirit (Rom. 8:9 ff. and II Cor. 3:17).[36]

Christ, then, was not revealed to Paul in a physical body, any more than he was to his disciples, or than he has been to those who have known him as Lord throughout the history of the church.

I cannot agree with Professor Knox that Paul " apparently discriminates between earlier and later appearances." [37] He writes that Paul must have had some " recognition of a difference in kind as between the initial experience of seeing the risen Christ, both the disciples' and his own, and ' visions ' of Christ which were still taking place." [38] Dr. Knox grants that "what this difference was we cannot know"; [39] but he suggests that "probably, on the human side, the difference lay in a feeling of complete matter-of-factness, as contrasted with the more ecstatic or visionary character of later appearances." [40] The implication of this supposition is that if there was a difference " on the human side " there must have been a corresponding difference on the divine side. The future implication is also made (by use of the terms " matter-of-factness " on the one hand, and " visionary " or " ecstatic " on the other) that the earlier appearances led to a more certain, and perhaps also a more complete and authentic, response to the resurrection than did the later appearances. I do not think, however, that early church history bears out the truth of such an inference. The author of the Fourth Gospel, who was undoubtedly not the disciple John, is nowhere listed as having seen Jesus in one of his earlier appearances; yet who could deny that Jesus appeared to him in as matter-of-fact and as vivid, complete, and authentic a way as he did to Paul? Is this not also true of Jesus' appearances to the martyrs and to those down through the centuries who have staked their lives on Christ's resurrection? I agree with Dr. Grant when he says, " In fact appearances of the risen Christ, especially to martyrs in the presence of death, but also to the devout in hours of exaltation, continued for a long time — indeed have never ceased in the long history of the church." [41]

The resurrection appearances to Paul, then, were of a revelatory rather than a historical nature, and Paul does not try to prove the resurrection by either materializing the form in which Jesus appeared, or by arguing that the tomb in which the body had been placed was empty. Paul does, however, use the appearances as proof of the resur-

rection, as Bultmann points out against Barth.[42] That
Paul makes such use of the appearances is clearly shown in
his remark that most of the "more than five hundred
brethren" to whom Jesus appeared "at one time" are
still living as he writes (I Cor. 15:6). Paul here implies
that the resurrection which he preaches can still be
checked; but in so using the appearances as evidence for
the fact of the resurrection, Paul takes the first step toward removing the resurrection out of the sphere of revelation and into the sphere of history. This process, perhaps
begun by Paul, was quickly developed by the church in
reaction against (Gnostic) heresies, and was completed by
the end of the New Testament period.

Soon after Paul's time, Jesus' appearances were materi-
alized and reported as having been of a physical nature.
Matthew, Luke, and John record them as such. Mark has
no account of any resurrection appearances, but only that
the tomb was empty and that Jesus could be seen in Galilee (Mark 16:1-8). He thus implies a physical resurrection. Matthew tells us that Mary Magdalene and "the
other Mary" met Jesus, "took hold of his feet and worshiped him" (Matt. 28:9), and that "the eleven disciples" also "saw him" (*idontes*) and worshiped him"
(Matt. 28:16 f.). It is stated clearly that Jesus appeared in
a physical form — that the women *took hold of his feet* —
and apparently he was recognized, both by the women and
later by the disciples, on sight. The appearances in Matthew are of a historical nature.

In Luke, however, the situation is somewhat different.
Some of the appearances there are completely physical,
while others are not. Luke seems to be midway in the development of historification between Paul and Matthew;
and here, as elsewhere, Luke reflects a stage in the devel-

opment of the tradition that is earlier than Matthew.[43] In Luke, Jesus bids his disciples to touch him, and asks them if they have anything to eat. He is then said to have eaten a piece of broiled fish (Luke 24:39, 41 ff.). He walked by the wayside (Luke 24:15 ff.), and broke bread (Luke 24:30). All this points to his appearance in a physical body — indeed in a body of flesh and bones. And yet there are in Luke's account several factors that imply a nonphysical appearance. These are:

1. The fact that the two men on the road to Emmaus did not recognize Jesus as he walked with them along the way. In the above-mentioned passages from Matthew and elsewhere in Luke (Luke 24:36 f.), Jesus is recognized as soon as he appears, as would have been the case had he appeared in flesh and blood; and yet on the road he was not recognized. Two different interpretations of the nature of the resurrection body seem to be represented here.

2. The fact that Jesus suddenly vanished out of the sight of the two disciples (Luke 24:31) implies that he appeared in a nonmaterial body.

3. The sudden appearance of Jesus in Jerusalem, standing among the disciples, suggested even to them that they were seeing "a spirit" (Luke 24:36 ff.).

4. Jesus' quick and final parting from the disciples (even if 24:51b is late) suggests a nonphysical body.

These ambiguities in Luke's account imply that the tradition recorded there was in a state of flux, Jesus being represented as having been raised in flesh and blood, yet not so certainly as in Matthew, for there are these indications in Luke that Jesus' resurrection appearances were not really made in genuine flesh and blood. Luke reveals the process of historification begun by Paul and completed by Matthew's time. It is clear that Jesus' resurrection appearances were not of a physical, historical nature (as they are generally represented to have been in the Gospels) but that the resurrection was known only by revelation. It could, therefore, not be demonstrated either by assurances that many witnesses still lived (as in I Cor., ch. 15), or by representing the appearances as having been made in flesh and blood so as to persuade the pagan world that there had been no mistake — that the resurrection had not been an illusion (as in the Gospels).

Two other factors supporting this thesis are the stories of the empty tomb and the ascension. The story of the empty tomb occurs in all four Gospels but not in Paul's account of the resurrection. This suggests that Paul either did not know it, or thought it too unconvincing or trivial to report. If he did not know it, it was probably because it had not yet been told; and if he thought it unconvincing or trivial, we shall concur in his judgment.

Our second-earliest source, Mark, reports that the three women who, alone in Mark, saw the empty tomb, were too afraid to tell anyone about it. Mark is here probably accounting for the fact that the story was late.[44] Moreover, according to Luke's report, the story seemed even to the apostles " an idle tale, and they did not believe " it (Luke 24:11). And this same reaction is reaffirmed at greater length by the two on the road to Emmaus (Luke 24:22 ff.). So also Mary, according to the Fourth Gospel, did not believe but wept, saying, " They have taken away my Lord " (John 20:11 ff.). Matthew tries to support the significance of the tomb's being empty by his story of the guards placed there and of their having been bribed to say that the body was stolen and had not really been raised. But this only reveals the defense that a person is led to set up as he retreats from the onslaughts to which he is subjected when he tries to demonstrate what is by nature undemonstrable. We conclude, therefore, that the empty tomb story was a later, unsuccessful attempt to prove as historical what could only have been known by revelation.

Finally, the ascension, whose date varies all the way from Easter Sunday in Luke, to forty days later in The Acts,[45] to twelve years later in *Pistis Sophia* and the *Book of Jeu*,[46] was a doctrine unknown at first, but later introduced to account for the disappearance of Jesus after he was represented as having been raised in a physical body.[47]

I therefore conclude with Bultmann that Jesus' resurrection was not a historical event — that is, of a verifiable character — as it would have been had he been raised a physical body. It appears, in the first place, that the New Testament accounts of the experience of the resurrection bear out this conclusion; and, in the second place, that Jesus' appearances in the flesh would not, in themselves, have been convincing. They would have been a matter of knowledge from which several conclusions could have been drawn (among which, that the body was stolen and revived), rather than a matter of faith from which only one conclusion could be deduced. They would, in short, have constituted history rather than revelation. But Jesus' resurrection was known only by revelation; he appeared only to those for whom its meaning had been prepared by a previous association with him; and, as the resurrection was known by revelation, it was a matter of faith that no logical argumentations or scientific data could either substantiate or refute.

We must note in conclusion that Jesus did not appear except to those who at his appearance identified him as Messiah.[48] No one else saw him. Why did no one else see him when he was raised? Many others besides his disciples

and those who believed in him had seen him before he
was crucified. In fact, the majority of those who saw him
did not believe; or if they believed, they did not do so for
long. The reason for this is that Jesus' earthly life and
crucifixion were historical in character and were suscep-
tible to many different interpretations — as *revealing* or as
not revealing. During Jesus' earthly life his Messiahship
was hidden from most eyes. Jesus' resurrection, however,
was of a different character. His Messiahship was not hidden in his resurrection; but it was precisely in his resurrection that it was revealed. To see Jesus as raised was at
the same time to accept Jesus as Lord, to believe.

We must also emphasize that the raised One was identified as *Jesus*. This means that no one saw Jesus as raised —
that is, believed he was the Messiah and accepted him as
Lord — except he also knew that Jesus had been crucified.
The raised One was the crucified One, who was Jesus.

The resurrection, then, had to be described in the
preaching, for, together with the crucifixion, it was the
center of the kerygma. Jesus had to be preached as crucified *and* as raised from the dead: " This Jesus . . . you
crucified. . . . But God raised him up." So preached Peter (Acts 2:23 f.). But *how* was the resurrection to be
preached? How was an event that had been known only by
revelation to be described? [49] The answer was, symbolically or mythologically. And the development of this description in the language of myth is, I believe, traceable
at least in outline form in the New Testament. The descriptions of the resurrection that are recorded in the New
Testament are, then, to be read and understood as mythological. They are not to be taken literally as though they
were self-authenticating accounts of a provable occurrence.

But because these stories are told mythologically (as I

agree with Bultmann they are) does it follow, as Bultmann concludes, that either (*a*) they point to no actual
occurrence in reality, or (*b*) they must be interpreted only
existentially? In order to answer these questions we must
first discuss the nature and function of myth.

CHAPTER VI

Mythology

DEFINITION OF MYTH

What is a myth? On the answer to this question there is a considerable difference of opinion. Bultmann defines myth as " that form of representation in which the other-worldly and divine appear as the worldly and human, the other side appears as this side. For example: in mythology God's otherworldliness is thought of in terms of spatial distance; and a cultic act is one in which a material medium conveys nonmaterial powers." [1]

Bultmann considers the whole framework of conceptions in which the kerygma is preached in the New Testament to be mythological — the cosmology presupposed (heaven, earth, and hell in three stories), the creation and Fall of Adam also presupposed, references to angels and demons, Jesus' pre-existence, the virgin birth, the resurrection and ascension, the Second Coming and the Last Judgment. He does not propose to strip away all this and preach simply what is left — this is the way the " modernists " take, which he rejects. He proposes, rather, to interpret all the kerygma that so lends itself in terms of existential philosophy; and he believes that in following this principle the permanent truth of the kerygma is preserved. Bultmann does not use " myth " to mean pure fiction. He defines it in the sense in which it has been used by most historians of religion, stressing the relativity of myths to their cultural origins and their subsequent obsolescence.

As a background against which Bultmann may be better understood, let us examine briefly the way in which mythology is understood and the way in which its origin is explained by the " history of religions " school. In the second half of the last century many scholars, notably philologists, undertook the study of comparative mythology. The predecessors of this school — the romantics — had, following Herder, usually believed mythology to have preceded language. They had referred to language as " faded mythology " and Schelling had concurred in this view. But scholars of the comparative mythology school adopted the methodological procedure of basing mythological comparisons on linguistic comparisons, thereby assuming the chronological priority of language to mythology; and mythology, which was not limited to that of the Greeks and Romans, was understood as " a part of a much more general phase through which all language has at one time or other to pass " [2] as well as less common " in these days of mature speculation." [3]

In order to understand more specifically this school's interpretation of mythology, let us note the findings of George W. Cox, published in 1881. In his introduction, Cox, like Max Müller, pointed to the primitive nature of myths when he said that " they constitute what in strict speech we may speak of as the whole learning of the people in early stages of thought and civilization, and sum up their thoughts on the origin and constitution of the outward world." [4]

Cox then attempted to account for the origin of myths. He believed that the growth of myths was determined by

that the immorality of the gods, thus arrived at accidentally, either grew out of or resulted in moral decadence
among the people, for he believed that " the mythology
of the Achaean or Greek people had very little to do with
their religion," [8] and that the religion and mythology of
the Greek poets must be absolutely separated.[9] Indeed, as
Greek religion " rose steadily to a higher standard," Greek
mythology " became more cumbrous, arbitrary, and re-
pulsive in its complications." [10]

It was believed, then, that mythological tales can always
be traced to phrases denoting sensible phenomena, and
that the changes that they underwent were due solely to
the failure of memory caused by the migration of tribes
from their ancient homes. So long as the names retained
their original meanings, connected stories could not be
put together; but when the meanings of the original
names describing sensible phenomena were forgotten, the
names then came to designate beings with human forms
and feelings, and mythology was born.

Cox was a historian of Aryan mythology, and almost the
same view of the origins of myths was taken by the philologist Max Müller. Professor Müller also believed that mythology was due to an inherent weakness of language and
that it could be made comprehensible only by a study of
the history of language. Mythology was, according to
Müller, " diseased language," being made up of metaphors
whose original, nonmetaphorical meanings were forgotten, and in place of which new meanings were inserted.
Wherever the stages of development between the original
and metaphorical meanings of words were artificially (and
not accurately) arrived at — there, according to Müller,
is mythology.[11] By mythology Müller refers to " all those
cases in which language assumes an independent power,

and reacts on the mind, instead of being, as it was intended to be, the mere realization and outward embodiment of the mind." [12]

Müller accounted for the origin of myths as Cox did. He believed that myths arose when it was forgotten that the same root word had previously described two different and distinct ideas. Thus, for example, the Sanskrit *arkâh,* meaning " light " or " ray of light," came to be used metaphorically as a name for the sun that gives light to the world, and as a description of a hymn of praise which brightens the faces of the gods. Later, the reason for " the independent bestowal of the same root on these two distinct ideas, sun and hymn, was forgotten . . . [and] we actually find in India that a myth sprang up, and that hymns of praise were fabled to have proceeded from, or to have originally been revealed by the sun." [13]

Mythology, according to this theory, came into being unconsciously and accidentally. It is not created nor is it considered to be a special medium by which truth can be communicated. Rather are myths considered to have emerged as errors to which later generations attempt vainly to attribute meaning. As myths, however, they contain no truth value, for they are the results of forgetfulness among more primitive peoples. Müller quotes with approval a definition of myth given by Professor Blackie in his article on mythology in Chambers' *Cyclopaedia:* a myth is " an unconscious act of the popular mind at an early stage of society " in distinction from an allegory which is " a conscious act of the individual mind at any stage of social progress." [14]

If myths are accidental offshoots of forgetfulness that do not really correspond to anything in reality, they would then seem to serve one of two purposes. Either they tell interesting stories whose meanings are not at all what they appear to be and have been lost unless the philologist can recapture them — in which case they are interesting only as revealing ancient or primitive ideas long since outgrown — or they may serve the purpose of providing etymologists with intriguing puzzles. But in any case they are illusions which can be explained only when the error from which they arose is discovered. Myths are said to have their origin in mental defects rather than in any positive creative power.

Bultmann's understanding of mythology reflects the influence of the thinking of such men as Müller and Cox. For Bultmann, also, New Testament myths (which are the only ones in which he is interested) are primitive errors which must be — not eliminated — but demythologized, i.e., interpreted existentially. Moreover, when Bultmann says at the conclusion of " Neues Testament und Mythologie," after he has referred to the favorable results of demythologizing, that the eschatological character of the saving event does not lend itself to secular proof,[15] he implies that the purpose of the myths has been to *prove*. It follows, then, for him, that mythology is irrelevant to the content of faith which is unprovable.

Bultmann makes this point quite explicitly later when he says, " It is precisely the fact that it is not provable which secures the Christian proclamation against the charge of being mythology." [16] Here Bultmann's understanding of the purpose of myth is clear: he believes that myths are intended to prove; that in mythology God is no longer transcendent, and the paradox of the transcendent God who is also immanent in history is destroyed. Bultmann believes, therefore, that by demythologizing he reasserts and reveals again the undemonstrable character of the Christian faith. But he has not rightly understood the purpose of myth, which is not to demonstrate or to prove, but to describe and portray.

In direct contrast to Bultmann stand Stählin and Sasse, both of whom deny that there are any myths in the New Testament. Stählin writes that myth " has no place on Biblical grounds," [17] and that everything in the Gospels and epistles is history.[18] Sasse states that " the New Testament does not need to be demythologized because it contains no myths." [19] But the problem with which Bultmann is dealing exists whether or not one calls the language of the New Testament mythological. To say that the New Testament contains no myths is, therefore, not to refute Bultmann but to evade the issue that he has raised.

Kümmel's criticism of Bultmann's definition is more to the point.[20] He argues that if myth is defined as broadly as Bultmann defines it, all the writings of the ancient world — including the New Testament — must be designated as mythological. Bultmann would undoubtedly agree, but his concern is to discover the present meaning, not of all ancient literature, but of the New Testament. Kümmel agrees that there is mythological language in the New Testament and he suggests using Martin Dibelius' definition of myths as " stories which tell somehow about the significant acts of the gods." [21] Kümmel would limit the definition of myth to include only deeds of a divine being in time and space that have definite meaning for man's existence.

Ernst Lohmeyer objects that what Bultmann calls myth is not only characteristic of the writings of the ancient world, but is also the language of all religions — ancient and contemporary. Thus Bultmann implicitly " condemns every religion to silence and, therefore, to nonexistence." [22]

But Bultmann does not so condemn Christianity to silence and nonexistence, because he does not consider God's act in Christ to be mythological "in the old sense" — that is, miraculous, supernatural, and dependent for its meaning upon a mythical world view. Lohmeyer also disagrees with Bultmann's definition of myth, and, in this regard, with Dibelius' definition to which Kümmel subscribes, in that he believes that mythology deals with more than God's relation to man — it also deals with God's relation to the world. Moreover, in its description of God and man, says Lohmeyer, myth says something not only about man, but also about God.[23] " The stories of creation are clear examples of myth." [24] Furthermore, it is not said that " God so loved *man* . . ." but that " God so loved the *world* that he gave his only Son." Thus mythology speaks not only about man's existence, but also about God and his relationship to the world.

In this I think we must concur so far as New Testament mythology is concerned, if it is agreed that New Testament mythology speaks about God and the world in a way that is related to man's existence. Mythological language about God also tells man something about himself. Thus, to use Lohmeyer's example, the story of creation is significant for Christian faith, not simply because it enlightens the believer about an activity of God in the distant past, but because it tells him that he is a creature who lives in a world that is created, and that, therefore, neither he nor the world in which he lives is able to procure his or its own salvation. And when New Testament mythology speaks about the world, it also tells man something about himself. To cite again Lohmeyer's example: Lohmeyer notes that John 3:16 says, not that God so loved *man*, but that God so loved the *world*. But what does John mean here by " the world "? He clearly means the world *of men,* for in v. 17 he states that the purpose of sending the Son was not to condemn the world but to save it, and in v. 18 he says that *he* who believes is not condemned but that *he* who does not believe is already condemned. John thus divides the " world " into two groups of men — believers and non-believers. Jesus came to save the *world,* and those *men* who believe are saved. Verse 19 shows further that by " the world " John means " the world of men " when he says that " the light has come into the *world,* and *men* loved darkness rather than light."

We should say, then, that New Testament mythology speaks about God in his relationship to man and to the world, and that everything it says about God or the world speaks to man in historical existence. Men do not read the New Testament in order to learn facts that do not concern their existence; but they read it in order the better to understand their own existence before God; and man's existence before God is always the same — a creature separated from the ground of his being, who longs for reconciliation.

New Testament mythology, then, does not merely describe a past event but points to an event that is always significant for the lives of men. There is a timeless quality about it. Lynn White writes, " A myth is not about something that once happened, but rather about something that is always happening: the narrative of an eternal event." [25] Brunner concurs when he says that so far as myth " expresses an event it is in the sense of something which continually recurs and which takes place always and everywhere "; [26] and Schelling arrived at the same point of view.[27]

Because New Testament mythology always tells man

something about his existence before God, it always demands that man make a decision — that he ask whether he will understand himself as a creature who did not create his own life, who cannot perpetuate it, and who can only receive it as he has in the past as a gift. Herein lies an important difference between New Testament and much pagan mythology, for the latter paints pictures but does not always call for decisions. As Brunner has said, " The Christian ' myth ' . . . is that way of thinking in which the Divine, the Eternal, the Absolute is not placed before us as a mere object of contemplation, but one in which the Absolute comes to us with a demand for decision." [28] Further, " The pagan myth . . . loves to gaze at the marvelous, to look at the amazing exploits of the gods, in which the only ' happening ' is an exhibition of the marvelous." [29] New Testament mythology never merely paints a picture to be looked at; it involves a new understanding of one's self and calls for decision.

Without, at this time, raising a question concerning the truth of mythology, we should define New Testament myths as dramatic stories in symbolic language, about God and his relation to men and the world, which demand of man a decision and a commitment. Most religious symbols are derived from mythology. This, says Urban, is " historically beyond question." [30] Further, the element of metaphor is always present in the symbol. Thus symbol and myth are closely related, symbol being the language in which the mythological tale is told. Brunner defines myth as " a symbol clothed in the form of an event, a substantive in verbal form." [31] In the following discussion " symbol " will be used in this sense.

MYTHOLOGY AND MODERN MAN

Having defined myth in the sense in which it is used in the New Testament, we realize with Bultmann that such language is today widely discredited. New Testament mythology is for many men difficult to understand, and in many areas has been rejected. This modern inability to understand mythology derives from the divorce between the imagination and the intellect which had its beginnings in the seventeenth century, especially in the persons of Descartes, Kepler, Bacon, and Hobbes. For Hobbes, for example, symbolic and metaphysical language had no place in serious discourse. The consequence was that poetry was interpreted as having no relation to " reality," religion declined into deism, and the truth value of myths was undermined.[32] In the case of the Biblical writings, modern literary and historical criticism contributed to the skepticism with which Biblical mythology was read. In short, the Biblical views of man, of history, and of the world, all of which are basic to the New Testament kerygma, have been affirmed to be outdated. Let us consider each of these views separately.

The New Testament describes man as seized by the Spirit or by demons. He is acted on by supernatural powers who hold sway over him, make of his life a battleground, and determine his destiny. The Spirit is said to have " snatched away " Philip after he had baptized the eunuch, so that when the eunuch came up out of the water he no longer saw Philip (Acts 8:39). Many modern men wonder what meaning such primitive animism can have for them; and yet, basic to the New Testament understanding of man is the belief that his life and destiny are only in a paradoxical way in his own hands. His freedom always rethe measure to which the old meaning of names was forgotten.[5] This, he believed, was the process:

First, a descriptive name was given to a natural phenomenon; and many such names were given, at different
times, to the same phenomenon describing it under different aspects. For example,

> The sun might be the wise being, the all-seeing, the wan
> derer, the toiler, the healer, the poisoner, the slayer, the
> short-lived, the beautiful, the malignant, the conqueror,
> the slave, the charioteer, the faithful, the faithless, the
> husband of the dew, the child or the destroyer of the
> night, the darkness, or the morning.[6]

The Greek word for this usage is " polyonymy."

Second, any of these words might be used as the basis of
a story about the sun.

Third, the crucial stage in the development of myth,
according to Cox, was the forgetting of the original meaning of the subject of the story. Indeed, when the original
meaning of the subject was forgotten, mythology came into
being. Thus when the meaning of Endymion as describing
the sun about to plunge into the sea was forgotten, " Endymion became a beautiful youth with whom the moon
fell in love, and whom she came to look upon as he lay in
profound sleep in the cave of Latmus." [7] Then the original
meaning of Latmus was also forgotten; at first meaning
only " forgetfulness," it came to designate a cave. And so
mythology was developed according to this pattern. Moreover, when the original meanings were lost, moral problems arose. Thus, for the Greek poet, the union of Selene
with Endymion — of the mother with the son — created
an immoral situation which was none the better because
it had arisen unconsciously. However, Cox did not believe

mains in a polar unity with the power of God.

The New Testament understands the meaning of history as revealed in a final way in Christ. It understands all preincarnation history as reaching its culmination in Christ; and all postincarnation history as participating in the eschatological age to which the Spirit has been given.[33] The coming of Christ is thus conceived as occurring at the mid-point of universal history; and history is thought of as a battleground on which supernatural forces are engaged in a struggle for mastery — God and his angels against Satan and his demons. At the mid-point of history God is victorious, but his victory is yet to be consummated at the Parousia. This view of history, which states its total meaning and its final destiny in terms of a central past event and a future total judgment and reconciliation, is widely thought to be highly presumptuous and naïve.

The world is assumed to be in three stories: heaven, earth, and hell. Christ's coming down from heaven to earth, his descent into hell, and his ascension back into heaven to be followed by his Second Coming are all based on this world view. But the view of the universe as a three-storied affair is demonstrably in error.

Because the New Testament view of man, history, and the world is mythological, it is today untenable by countless thoughtful men and women throughout the world who, like Bultmann and his predecessors, can see no truth value in mythology as it stands. This distrust of myth has its ultimate origin in the belief that nothing is real except that which is given for man to perceive through his senses. It is conceded that language has a reality of its own, but that it is valuable only as a reflecter of sensible phenomena — as a description of things and occurrences in the natural world. Everything that man creates is thought to be an imitation of something else that is given, reflecting reality but only an illusion as compared with it. Language — nonmythological as well as mythological — becomes in the end a subjective falsification of sensibly presented realities, for language is not given to the senses, but is created.

However, if nothing is real except sensibly presented phenomena, then not only is mythology and all other language an illusion, but so also are all the arts and all theoretical knowledge. In the case of the arts, they are all human creations and " imitations "; they merely represent and have no independent content and no intrinsic meaning. And theoretical knowledge, according to this view, like the arts and language, represents reality in concepts; it is not reality itself but merely reflects reality.

Yet is it possible for us to agree that reality can be understood as consisting only of sensibly presented phenomena, only of that with which nature presents us? Is not any representation in language, the arts, or knowledge, as real as what is represented? It may not be as true, as beautiful, or as good; but it is certainly as real. Representations, as soon as they come into being, are independent realities with their own content and their own meaning. Stuart's portrait of Washington is a representation; but it is a part of reality as surely as George Washington himself was. The painting may not be true, i.e., it may not represent Washington as he really was; and it may not be beautiful; but it is certainly real.

The same is true in the realms of music and the dance. Beethoven's quartets, Flagstad's *Isolde,* or Markova's *Giselle* — all artistic representations — are unforgettably real to anyone who has seen or heard them, and caught a glimpse of that to which they have pointed. In the same way, all language, including mythology, is real. Once a word or tale or myth has come into being, it has become a new and additional part of reality; it has assumed an independent existence. Summarizing this point, Ernst Cassirer has written:

> Myth, art, language, and science appear as symbols; not in the sense of mere figures which refer to some given reality by means of suggestion and allegorical renderings, but in the sense of forces each of which produces and posits a world of its own. . . . Instead of taking them as mere copies of something else, we must see in each of these spiritual forms a spontaneous law of generation; an original way and tendency of expression which is more than a mere record of something initially given in fixed categories of real existence. . . . Thus the special symbolic forms are not imitations, but *organs* of reality.[34]

And as Cassirer says in another place, " The word, like a god or daemon, confronts man not as a creation of his own, but as something . . . in its own right, as an objective reality." [35] " The inner excitement which was a mere subjective state has vanished, and has been resolved into the objective form of myth or of speech." [36]

Another factor that has tended to undermine faith in the New Testament message has been the belief that worlds other than our own are inhabited, each with its own history, its own time, its own sin, and its own need of redemption. Then, are there other histories of which Christ is not the center? Or are there other worlds that Christ will not save? If there are, then God has either left them without means of salvation, or salvation is possible outside of Christ. Or, must the Logos be reincarnated? And if he must, the crucifixion was not once-for-all, the uniqueness of time and history is given up, and " Christ is become Krishna of the myriad incarnations." [37] In 1600, Giordano Bruno, the first preacher of "the infinity of worlds," was sent to the stake. Is there no other way by which the church can defend its proclamation? White concludes:

> The new astronomy had undermined confidence in the uniqueness of the incarnation; the new biology destroyed the symmetry of Christian history which had been designed to explain that incarnation. Consequently, in the opinion of many men, the entire structure collapsed, and faith in the singleness and purpose of the time-process waned. . . . To many devout and intelligent Christians the present crisis marks the end of Christianity.[38]

MYTHOLOGY AND UNIVERSAL PERSPECTIVES

What position is the church to take in such a situation? Can it preach its message in nonmythological language? Is Bultmann right in his belief that the New Testament kerygma can be preserved and perpetuated meaningfully if it is divorced from its mythological framework and reinterpreted in the language of contemporary existentialist philosophy? The language of the latter is demonstrably intelligible to increasing numbers of men, especially in Europe; but can it contain and reproduce the New Testament proclamation?

I believe the answer to these questions must be "No," for it appears that aside from the question of whether or not New Testament mythology is true, the basic claim of the New Testament that in Christ all men may be saved cannot be stated except in the language of myth. If there is only one God who revealed himself once-for-all in Jesus Christ, then Christ must have universal significance and must be preached in a universal framework. Indeed, the incarnation is understandable only if it is related to the

Fall and final destiny of man. But to relate Christ to universal history is necessarily to speak mythologically, for such history is not immediately perceived and observed and cannot be described, but is imaginatively conceived and must be described mythologically.

It is precisely the comprehensive, universal world view of the Bible which is most difficult for modern man to believe: God as the beginning and the end — the Creator and Redeemer, and the centrality of Israel, Christ, and the church for the salvation of the whole race. All this is rejected as "mere myth," tied up to first-century ideas, and no truer or less true than the claims of other religions. Yet the whole meaning of Christ depends upon his having just this significance: if Christ is *my* Savior, then he must be the Savior of *all;* but if he is not the latter, he cannot be the former. Christ came either to redeem the world or he did not come to save at all. If he is Savior, he must be related to Alpha and Omega, to creation as well as to redemption, and to the beginning and end of every human life and of everything that is or ever shall be.[39] Such integration of ultimates as is made in the New Testament is possible only in symbolic language.

Wide perspectives are not, of course, the exclusive possession of religion in general or of Christianity in particular. The artist also integrates various elements of experience into an organic whole. But faith extends this integrating process to ultimates, resolving the contradictions of all human life and history into a meaningful whole. Reinhold Niebuhr writes:

> Religion seeks mythically to grasp life in its unity and wholeness. This unity and wholeness can never be expressed in terms of complete rationality, for reason only observes and deduces. What it observes is concrete reality

in its multifarious forms. Its deductions are based upon the sequences that it observes in nature and history. But these sequences reveal nothing of the internal unity in all organic growth. For this reason scientific descriptions of reality always tend to a mechanistic interpretation of it. The facts of organic growth can be comprehended and described only by mythically transferring the inner unity of the human consciousness (where unity is directly experienced and apprehended) to the external world. A certain amount of primitive myth is always involved in this process (its analogy to animism of primitive mythology is apparent). But it is also permanent myth in the sense that it is permanently valid, since reality is actually organic and not mechanical in its processes.[40]

This integrating process is the task of faith which, in its dealings with universal perspectives, goes beyond the poet's horizon. " The poet . . . describes always some definite particular and individual situations. . . . Only indirectly does he grope for the mystery of the All." The man of faith, on the other hand, " has this mystery as his direct object," writes Dr. Kroner.[41] And the insights of faith are gained only by personal and communal wrestling with the ambiguities, and contradictions, and meaninglessness of life and history on the one hand, and by an encounter with God on the other.[42] Revelation is given through this struggle, and a single perspective of past, present, and future, of God and of history, of creation at the beginning and of redemption at the end. This insight into the transcendent source of the meaning of life cannot be scientifically described, because it is not externally observed or scientifically arrived at. Myth is the only language in which such a vision, which sees heaven and earth, the beginning and the end all at once, can be expressed; for these are not seen upon scientific investigation, but only upon an encounter, at a profound level of experience, with the vicissitudes of life. It is through this encounter that God appears. Such an integrating vision requires its own means of expression, quite different from the language that describes specific observations; and this medium is myth.

During the reign of the emperor Julian, the Neoplatonist Sallustius wrote of myth that " the mind sees the whole process at once, words tell of part first, part second." [43] Symbolic words must separate and tell in a sequence what the mind sees as a unity. Mozart is said to have written to a friend that in his " mind " or " imagination " (*im Geist*) he heard a whole composition, not in its successive parts but " all at once "; and he added that this was " decidedly the best way." [44] However, he had to set down the composition note by note in order to represent as accurately as he could what he had heard; but he preferred hearing not note by note but " all at once." In much the same way, mythology is the medium by which faith represents in a dramatic sequence what it has seen as a unity.[45]

We have said that *only* the language of myth can convey the content of myth. As neither scientific investigation nor discursive reasoning can arrive at that which myth describes, so neither the language of science nor that of logical propositions can convey meanings that lie outside the spheres of scientific and logical inquiry. On this point White well says:

> Although one may discuss a myth, one can never completely convey or explain its content in any other medium, because in the best myths dramatic presentation still leaves many meanings compounded in a counterpoint of significance which is destroyed by further analysis.[46]

Furthermore, a myth and its object become united to the point that what the myth says cannot be said precisely in any other language. This is also true of poetry; but it is not true of discursive language where words stand in a mediating position, " establishing relationships between the given phenomenon and others which are ' like ' it." [47] Mythic thinking, on the other hand, does not relate and classify but brings what it refers to into the present, and is " merged with its object in an indissoluble unity." [48] If one attempts to transpose the content of myth into non-symbolic language, the symbolic meaning, which it was precisely the purpose of the myth to convey, cannot any longer be communicated. As Urban has said, if a myth is reduced to " bare reality," it becomes an illusion; " it is stripped of all the accumulated intention which it is precisely the function of the symbols to retain." [49] And Reinhold Niebuhr has put it this way:

> A completely rationalized myth loses its virtue because it ceases to point to the realm of transcendence beyond history, or, pointing to it, fails to express the organic and paradoxical relationship between the conditioned and the unconditioned.[50]

Whether or not, then, New Testament mythology describes objective truth, we must conclude that its meanings cannot be communicated in any other language.

We have noted that modern man prefers generally to rely on scientific language for what he can accept as truth. The symbols used in science are more readily believed than those used in poetry and religion; and Christian myths are commonly frowned upon as quaint and primitive stories, which do not describe what can be accepted as objective truth, but are better understood as subjective

responses in the ancient world to very personal circumstances. The problem of New Testament language is frequently complicated when it is referred to as " mythological " in character because of the erroneous conception
of myth as pure fancy. Berdyaev wrote:

> It is high time that we stopped identifying myth with
> invention, with the illusions of primitive mentality, and
> with anything, in fact, which is essentially opposed to
> reality. For that is the sense which we give the words
> " myth " and " mythology " in ordinary conversation.[51]

There is, for example, a moth preventive that is adver-
tised by these words: " Makes a myth of moths." But aside
from such current use of the word " myth," the New Testament message is believed with increasing qualms of conscience because of the common notion that truth can be
expressed only by scientific language and nonpoetic, discursive reasoning due to the supposed empirical nature of
reality. The question, then, is: Is mythological language
ever true? Does it ever point to objective reality? We are
here particularly concerned with New Testament mythology.

The modern difficulty in believing myths of any kind
stems from the separation (which has existed since the
seventeenth century) of the intellect from the imagination, of the mind from the feelings. The intellect or the
mind is looked upon as capable of arriving at objective
truth, whereas the imagination and the senses are not. As
a result of this divorce, theologians have often defended
the kerygma by taking one of two courses: either they
have conceded to the opposition by relinquishing the
mythology and stressing Christian ethics and its similarity
to the ethics of other religions; or they have rather defi-

antly insisted on the literal truth of all New Testament myths by resorting to a Biblicism that has made no attempt to relate the language and content of faith to those of science.

In more recent times, semantics, esthetics, philosophy and religion are beginning to see the impossibility of maintaining either of these extreme positions. It is being more frequently realized that a symbol has a right to be *interpreted,* and need not be either discarded or simply repeated verbatim; but it must be interpreted in terms of the reality that it describes. We must be willing to grant that the symbol user knows, although perhaps imperfectly, what he means. How, then, does a symbol say what it means? To quote Urban again: It endows

> an occurrence in space and time with a meaning to which greater value or significance is given than belong to it in its pure actuality or existence. The essential character of all symbolism, in its primary form, is that images or ideas are taken from narrower and more intuitible relations and used as *expressions* for more ideal and universal relations which, because of their very pervasiveness and ideality, cannot be either directly intuited or expressed.[52]

These " images " or " ideas," which " cannot be either directly intuited or expressed," are created and perceived by the imagination which is a unifying function of the mind. The imagination unifies what is known by experience through clues, and is undemonstrable. Dr. Kroner has defined the imagination as a " synthesis of opposites; namely, of the opposites of sensation and reason, of receptivity and spontaneity, of the empirical and the speculative, of experience and creativity." [53] We have said that these images are, in part, " created "; but this does not mean that they are pure fancy, for the imagination is determined partly by the objective reality of what is sensed, and partly by the referral of the image to previous knowledge. The existential truth of what is imagined is constantly subject to verification by experience.

Moreover, it is only by his use of the religious imagination that man is able to meet what might otherwise be overpowering ambiguities and inequalities and tragedies of his life. Richard Kroner writes that " the insolubility of the ultimate problem and the exigency of the practical purpose unite thus in the postulate of religious imagination." [54] Man's experience sometimes forces him up against a vision that is real for him, the reality of which no one else can deny, but which others may affirm as also true for them. This mystical intuition of reality is articulated by the religious imagination — not precisely, but symbolically. " Words like ' God,' ' paradise,' ' angel,' ' heaven,' ' creation,' ' grace ' . . . are not well-defined; on the contrary, they are enveloped in a mist. . . . Their logical weakness is just their religious strength." [55] And faith cannot survive apart from the insights of imagination; for it is the imagination which makes visible the invisible elements with which faith deals. " Imagination . . . [makes] visible what is invisible, and [detects] the invisible element in the visible situation ": [56]

> There was a time when meadow, grove, and stream,
> The earth, and every common sight,
>   To me did seem
>   Apparelled in celestial light,
> The glory and the freshness of a dream.[57]

The imagination articulates the invisible, the transcendent; and, as Marcel urges, the transcendent is not a break with experience but a deepening of the implications of experience.[58] Man innately reaches out toward the transcendent. " The world of utensils, other men, and history is insufficient to satisfy the expansive urge of the self for a perfective union with the other in being. The attitude of transcending is ultimately founded on a nisus to reach beyond the world as a whole." [59]

Myth is the articulation of what is created and perceived by the imagination, but is not logically demonstrable. Myths are believed in faith; and although they cannot be proved to be true by the reason, they are accepted, by reason, as pointing to truth. In defending the truth of myths, Niebuhr writes:

> The transcendent source of the meaning of life is thus in such relation to all temporal process that a profound insight into any process or reality yields a glimpse of the reality which is beyond it. This reality can be revealed and expressed only in mythical terms. These mythical terms are the most adequate symbols of reality because the reality which we experience constantly suggests a center and source of reality, which not only transcends immediate experience, but also finally transcends the rational forms and categories by which we seek to apprehend and describe it.[60]

A very good example of the limitation of scientific language and of the necessity of using the language of myth is to be seen in the myth of creation. Scientific language can only describe various processes of life and history and under what circumstances certain forms have been transmuted into other forms. " But it can only describe these processes after the fact, and it is forced to treat each new emergent as following necessarily from the forces which immediately preceded it." [61] Science, then, cannot affirm the myth of creation. Cause and effect is not equivalent to creation, for the latter presupposes freedom and alternative whereas the former presupposes recurrence. Science cannot speak of a Creator but only of a cause of the universe. But this latter phrase is self-contradictory. Either the cause lies outside the universe, in which case the universe is not the All, and there remains a supernatural realm of reality with which science cannot deal; or the cause is part of the universe, in which case it is not a cause. "The myth of creation" therefore "expresses dynamic . . . qualities in reality which cannot be stated in rational terms." [62]

Mythology is not a pseudoscience stemming from the childhood of the race, but is a unique way of apprehending reality.[63] Myths are indispensable to Christianity because it is only from the language of mythology that symbols are taken, and the real insights of Christianity (as of every religion) can be expressed only symbolically. The language and symbolism of science were created for another purpose. And myths are indispensable also because it is only from mythology that Christianity gets its dramatic language which is necessary in the communication of its basic truths. Without mythology one is left with an intellectual abstraction wherein the quality of the dramatic is totally absent; and Christian truth cannot be proclaimed without the aid of dramatic language. (By dramatic language is meant not primarily language of emotion, but language of action.) Myths, told in dramatic language, symbolize and point to metempirical reality, which cannot be described by the mathematical-logical language of science. Without dramatic language theology loses touch with religion.

It was precisely for this reason that Plato, although he did not make a rigorous distinction between the language of science and that of mythology, turned to the dramatic language of myth to point to cosmologically significant truth that he could not describe in a more exact language. Mythology was not, in Plato's case, a language that had later to be displaced in the interest of accuracy; but, to the contrary, Plato deliberately chose the more inexact language of mythology in the interest of expressing what he believed to be truth.

Religion cannot exist without myth; and, as Berdyaev says:

> Myth is a reality immeasurably greater than concept. . . . Behind the myth are concealed the greatest realities, the original phenomena of the spiritual life. The creation of myth among peoples denotes a real spiritual life, more real indeed than that of abstract concepts and of rational thought. . . . Myth presents to us the super-natural in the natural, the supra-sensible in the sensible, the spiritual life in the life of the flesh; it brings two worlds together symbolically.[64]

The significance of myth, as well as its necessity in communication, is vividly expressed by Milton C. Nahm, primarily in connection with art; but what he says about symbols used in art is equally true of religious symbols. He writes:

> These images live, not in the "faith of reason," but in the life of feeling which is, in part, recognitive and reproductive. Art gains familiarity because of this, and the arts display the principle in the recurrence of symbols — symbols of the hunt and the chase, of danger and vengeance, chicanery, death, old age, change, tales of marriage, of spring and winter, the passage of time and of the seasons, chance and love, the ladder and the tree of life, the isles of the blest, the demons and the werewolves of a hundred Beowulfs and Homers, tales of horror, the

storied fables of the beneficence of warm sun and soft rain, of the mating of earth and heaven, the havoc of storm, hurricane, and earthquake, of plague, pestilence, starvation, and war. From this I conclude that by the relation of feeling to generic signs we search for communication and its means only to find them " tumbling at our feet " in the permanent record of feelings which men symbolize in their art.[65]

The fact that the imaginative truth of Christianity has also been expressed in symbols that have lived on and been repeated for centuries, and in many cultures, testifies to their service to unchanging human feelings. The church also searches for means of communication only to find them tumbling at its feet in the permanent record of the symbolic language of its heritage. These symbols must correspond to an order of experience that is real — that has been known and affirmed by people of many races, cultures, and backgrounds, of all levels of education, experience, and accomplishment, for century after century. Is not this testimony an argument for the meaningfulness of these myths and the truth to which they point? It is a historical fact, which we cannot lightly pass over, that these symbols have connoted undemonstrable truth to which the widest variety of men have assented, century after century. These myths have communicated meanings that have been immediately recognized and identified, and they continue to do so today when they are rightly interpreted. At the proclamation of these myths it is shown that " the primitive worshiper and the mystical saint are brothers under their skins and find it natural to use a common imagery and a common speech." [66]

THE INTERPRETATION OF MYTHS

We believe, then, that myths are indispensable in the communication of the Christian message, but that they must be interpreted because they do not speak an exact language. As the language of myth is transcended by the content of myth, myths cannot be interpreted literally. When they are so interpreted, they no longer describe what they were intended to represent. From a literal point of view, myths are inaccurate. Dr. Niebuhr states this characteristically when he writes:

> As Clutton-Brock observed, religion is forced to tell many little lies in the interest of a great truth, while science inclines to tell many little truths in the interest of a great lie. The great truth in the interest of which many little lies are told is that life and history have meaning and that the source and the fulfillment of that meaning lie beyond history. The great lie in the interest of which science tells many little truths is that spatiotemporal realities are self-contained and self-explanatory and that a scientific description of sequences is an adequate analysis of causes.[67]

> A portrait is mythical as compared with the scientific exactitude of a photograph. Though a wise photographer will try to catch the permanent and significant rather than the passing mood of his subject, he is always limited by the physical facts. The artist, on the other hand, falsifies some of the physical details in order to arrive at a symbolic expression of the total character of his subject, this total character being a transcendent fact that is never completely embodied in any given moment of the subject's existence. A really great portrait will go beyond this, and symbolizes not only the transcendent personality of the subject but will contain suggestions of a universal human mood.[68]

As soon as a myth is scientifically analyzed and broken down into its several parts, its meaning is lost. Eichrodt's

comment on the presence of God in fire in the Old Testament illustrates the point. In his great *Theologie des Alten
Testaments,* he says:

> It is idle to dispute as to whether in Israel men believed
> that they really saw God himself in such natural phe-
> nomena, or whether they thought they had seen God
> only figuratively speaking, as in a picture. Popular
> thought usually makes no such ingenious theological dis-
> tinctions; and in Israel, at any rate, the seeing of God
> was certainly very real. The best proof for this is the
> record of the covenant meal on Mt. Sinai at which
> Moses and the seventy elders of the people saw Israel's
> God. . . . But that the divine glory is in reality inde-
> scribable is shown by the complete absence of any de-
> tailed description of Yahweh's face or form, which are
> characterized only as a brilliant light.[69]

Such myths are figures of speech used to convey experienced realities that cannot be exactly described or de-
noted, but are rather connoted in tropes. In myths there
are deviations from reality, and the religious consciousness knows the myths to be symbolic; it perceives a difference between form and meaning. It knows that it is using
the mythical to symbolize the nonmythical and that the
myth both is and is not what it represents. This is also
true with poetic symbols: for Shelley, the skylark both
was and was not a bird. The literal meaning, then, of a
religious symbol does not constitute its inner or essential
truth, but the symbol must be interpreted. A great portrait cannot be understood by an analysis of its deviations
from reality, but only if it is viewed with the same imaginative vision that characterized the artist who painted it.
This is as true in all the arts as it is in religion; and Christian myths cannot be interpreted by scientific standards
but only through eyes of faith. The myth must be " broken " from history and understood as a sign pointing from

the temporal to the beyond.[70]

Although the myth points to a reality to which no other form of expression can allude, paradoxically, in interpreting the myth, the very language that cannot describe the truth to which the myth points *must* be used. The myth must then be repeated after it has been interpreted, and one must understand the myth in the light of the interpretation, and not the interpretation in the light of the myth.

But *how* are New Testament myths to be interpreted? Is there a principle that can be applied to them all, and by which they can be made understandable even to modern men trained in the most exact sciences? Bultmann has proposed such a principle. He believes that in order to communicate the New Testament kerygma to modern men we must strip it, not of certain myths, but of the whole mythological framework in which the New Testament casts the kerygma. It is his view, further, that when the core of the kerygma is interpreted existentially, it is in that moment delivered from its mythological structure; and then contemporary man is enabled to appropriate to himself its authentic and abiding significance. Bultmann's principle of interpretation is thus to demythologize and interpret existentially. Is this principle adequate?

On behalf of this principle it must be said that it has put us all in debt to Bultmann for a profound elaboration of one aspect of the New Testament kerygma. But, against this principle, it must be noted that by interpreting New Testament mythology only in terms of what it means to the individual, here and now, one silently eliminates from consideration all language (mythological or not) that is not intended primarily to deal with the *individual, here and now*. Too much of the New Testament is thus condemned to silence; and this is precisely what happens to

would be true of *any* principle applied. What is important, however, is that no principle of interpretation be adopted that is inherently unable, when applied, to lead to meaningful exegesis of the whole. We do not advocate obscurantism; neither do we believe, however, that elimination is the only alternative.

We have spoken of Bultmann's existential interpretation of the kerygma and agreed that Bultmann has elaborated an authentic aspect of the New Testament proclamation. He focuses his attention primarily on the crucifixion-resurrection, and interprets it existentially. But we must say something now about the matter of " existential " interpretation. In the first place, it is incorrect to assume that only those aspects of the kerygma that have primarily an existential, or anthropological reference are understandable — unless, that is, one defines " existential " so broadly as to include " understandable " in its meaning, in which case anything understandable has, *eo ipso,* been interpreted existentially. Likewise, if by an " existential " interpretation of Scripture is meant an interpretation that may be received as having meaning for man in historical existence, then clearly all interpretation of Scripture must be " existential," and one should attempt to interpret only such mythological data as may be interpreted existentially. But Bultmann interprets only the data whose *primary* reference is to the individual believer caught in the vicissitudes of historical existence. It appears that the *only* question he asks of Scripture is: What does this mean for me, here and now? This orientation to Scripture is clearly stated when he writes, " The question of God and the question of myself are identical." [71] But if the individual's first question is consistently, What does this have to do with me? he will find himself (as does Bultmann) elimi-

nating rather than augmenting the areas that have to do
with himself. By a too steady focusing on the self, man
shrivels rather than grows; and likewise by a too steady
search for an immediately applicable interpretation of the
mythology of the New Testament kerygma to himself, here
and now, the individual will be increasingly unable to appropriate more and more of the kerygma as in *any* sense
meaningful. Like poetry, only to a far greater degree, New
Testament mythology draws a man out of himself, and
points him *beyond* himself as well as *to* himself; and he
may even *find* himself by looking away, by " losing " his
life.

It must also be added that in his overconcern with what
the gospel says to the individual, Bultmann quite ignores
the concept of the church, which is so pervasive in the
New Testament, where the believer is a believer only in
the context of the church, and he functions, qua believer,
as a member of the body of Christ. The believer's orientation, therefore, is not just to Christ, but also to his brothers in Christ, and to those outside the church whom he
seeks to bring in. Bultmann's strongly individualistic emphasis on the isolated believer and his concern for self-
understanding does not do justice to the New Testament's
equally strong emphasis on the church and on the *koinōnia.*

This emphasis of Bultmann's, which is not the all-
predominating emphasis of the New Testament, is related
to his use of Heidegger's analysis of human existence.
Heidegger believes that the categories usually used to describe things in the world are inappropriate to describe
man's existence; and so he describes possible ways of being, the most fundamental of which are " authentic " and
" inauthentic " existence. Inauthentic existence is exist-

ence in anonymity, and is impersonal. Authentic existence, on the other hand, involves the achievement of self-
hood, the declaration of individuality. It is never fully
attainable, however, for what is ultimately determined is
death.

Heidegger's analysis of existence as " inauthentic " or
" authentic " is seen by Bultmann to be similar to the New
Testament's understanding of man as " natural " or " spiritual," as not " in Christ " or as " in Christ," as " outside of
faith " or as " in faith." But the New Testament emphasis
is not on individual resolvedness in separation from man,
but is rather on corporate, community existence in Christ,
or with Christ as the head. Of course it is true, and Bultmann is quite right when he emphasizes that *individual*
life is not lost but is fulfilled in Christ; but individual life
is fulfilled, according to the New Testament, in a *corporate*
life, in the church, and *only* in this corporate life. It is the
New Testament's emphasis on the significance, nay the *in-
dispensability* for salvation of participation in the *koinōnia*
that Bultmann has failed to grasp. Here he is truer to
Heidegger than to the kerygma he seeks to proclaim. In
the New Testament, individuality is always in polarity
with community, and the church must always be on guard
lest one or the other be overemphasized. Bultmann's theology stands in danger of becoming a phenomenology of
faith — if, in fact, it is not quite that.

Bultmann's demythologization has led him, then, to
eliminate a good part of the kerygma — all that he is not
able to demythologize. He maintains that the core of the
kerygma is preserved, and this may be true; but the elaboration of this core in a wider framework is given up. The
meaning of the crucifixion — and only one meaning at
that — becomes, for him, the meaning of the kerygma.

We would suggest that with all the variety of approach and of understanding to be found in the New Testament, the book is still basically a unity. Jesus Christ as Savior of men is at its center. This central object reflects light, like a well-cut diamond, from innumerable prisms; but each reflection, stemming from the same source, is genuine and authentic. The New Testament is the record of the varied responses that were made to many reflections of light; and in Part Three we shall elaborate at greater length our proposal for interpreting existentially some of the varied aspects of New Testament theology that are expressed in the language of myth.

Kümmel has suggested that border statements be critically examined, and that perhaps some New Testament myths which are on the periphery of the kerygma might be eliminated in the interest of clarifying the kerygma as a whole.[72] But there could never be agreement as to which myths are meaningless and obsolete because *none* of them is universally either meaningless or outdated. For example: Kümmel states that the thousand-year world rule prophesied in the Apocalypse does not stand in continuity with the central message of the New Testament, but, on the contrary, contradicts the words of Jesus found in Luke 17:21. Cullmann, on the other hand, finds the thousand-year reign also in Paul (I Cor. 15:23 ff.) and defines it as the last act of the reign of Christ.[73] Thus the myth has meaning for Cullmann, as it apparently does not have for Kümmel, and Cullmann finds it to be a genuine part of the kerygma as Kümmel does not. All the individual should say, then, about any particular New Testament myth, is that it has no meaning for him; he cannot say that it has no meaning in itself — for anyone. The theologian should attempt to elaborate meanings in continuity with the intention of the author and with an understanding of the many interpretations that the history of the church supplies; but he cannot pass any final judgment on whether or not any meaning exists. It is to be granted that there are both central and peripheral meanings in the New Testament; but it cannot be conceded that any New Testament " doctrine " is, in itself, meaningless.

One part of the New Testament is often used as normative for another part, or Scripture is approached with an a priori test. So, for example, Luther discovered a gospel within the gospel and rejected whole canonical books as normative for him, as representing the kerygma.[74] This raises the larger question of the authority of the Bible which we shall not pursue here but which is the subject of Chapter XIII. Let it suffice for the present to quote in this connection some words that Irenaeus once wrote of Marcion — namely, that he " has persuaded his disciples that he himself is truer than those apostles who delivered the gospel; so that he delivers to them not the gospel, but a bit of the gospel." [75] The church has not been given the authority to preach " bits " of the gospel. It must preach first things first; but it must preach, as far as it is able, the *whole* gospel. Heresy consists in preaching a part as if it were the whole; but it is only the *whole* gospel that makes whole.

VII

New Testament Mythology

CATEGORIES OF MYTHS

In the preceding chapter, having defined myth, we then elaborated on the difficulty that modern man has in either understanding or accepting New Testament mythology; but we concluded that as the Christian faith deals with universal perspectives, and as only the language of myth is able to describe such perspectives, Christianity cannot be communicated apart from that language. We then tried to show that New Testament myths point to, but do not accurately describe, objective truth; that these myths must be interpreted in terms of their original meanings, and that the church should never set one myth against another for the purpose of eliminating one of them, for the church has no criterion by which to eliminate any part of the only medium by which uniquely it knows its Lord. Or, to put it another way: all New Testament myths should be preserved as part of the kerygma, but they must be interpreted to man in terms that elaborate their original intention and that will help him to understand the meaning of his life, the way in which alone it is fulfilled, and the destiny that it is promised.

All New Testament myths, therefore, contribute to the meaning of the kerygma. But we must also recognize that

115

the New Testament contains myths of several different kinds. Indeed, there appear to be three different kinds of myth in the New Testament: (*a*) those myths which refer to purely metahistorical events; (*b*) those which refer to events that are partly historical and partly metahistorical; and (*c*) those which refer to historical events. By " metahistorical myths " I mean myths that cannot be understood as referring to events that have occurred or are to occur in the realm of history. By " history " I mean the time of our lives, the plane on which life is lived from birth to death. There are in the New Testament myths that cannot be thought of as taking place on this plane, that never enter into the physical existence of man between birth and death. There are other myths that may be understood as partly metahistorical and partly historical; and there are still others that have meaning only in relation to history — to the period of our lives.

According to the New Testament understanding of history, however, all its myths are considered as " historical," for " history " in the New Testament sense includes events that were not or will not be experienced by men in the flesh. In other words, the New Testament considers as *historical*, events that we shall refer to as *metahistorical*. In order better to understand the meanings of various New Testament myths, we shall make a distinction that the New Testament does not make, differentiating between those myths which are to be considered as referring to events that have taken place or may only be thought of as to take place in the lives of men in flesh and blood, here on this earth; and those myths which may be only understood as having occurred or as to occur *outside* of the realm of human, historical existence as we know it. We refer to the former as " historical," and to the latter as

" metahistorical." There are, in addition, certain myths, which overlap these two categories, that are both metahistorical and historical in character. Let us now see which myths fall into each category.

METAHISTORICAL MYTHS

There arc, in the first place, myths, which describe states or events of the past or future, that cannot be thought of as occurring in the realm of history as we have defined it. They are purely metahistorical in nature, but in the New Testament they are conceived of as occurring in space and time — the New Testament describing all events as though they were events in time, and understanding heaven and hell as " places " in space. These myths, then, are understood in the New Testament as historical in nature, although the ones that are described as having taken place in the past are not believed to have been witnessed by men. These, however, we classify as metahistorical.

Furthermore, it is only the myths of this first class that refer to events yet to take place, and these events also are depicted in the New Testament as of a historical character. The myths of this class are the most obviously mythological in nature because of the fact that they are altogether metahistorical. We must now consider the myths and mythological data that fall into this group.

1. *Heaven and Hell.* In the New Testament, heaven and hell are presupposed and understood as places in the realm of space; but they are mythological in character and metahistorical in the sense that, except figuratively speaking, they are never known or experienced in historical existence. They are, however, historified and literalized in the New Testament, as was the case in all literature written

the New Testament when Bultmann's principle of interpretation is applied to it. One does not question the fact that the gospel preached when it has been demythologized is both authentic and understandable; but it is fragmentary. And we cannot accept any principle of hermeneutics that rules out significant areas of the New Testament as no longer able to say anything meaningful. Bultmann's principle precludes in advance the possibility of appropriating the wider dimensions of the kerygma which can be articulated only in the mythological terms in which the New Testament represents them. It is my belief, in the first place, that more of the kerygma may be interpreted with an existential meaning than Bultmann concedes (see Part Three) ; and, in the second place, that modern man *is* able to understand mythological language even if its primary reference is not an existential or anthropomorphic one.

The mythological framework in which the kerygma appears in the New Testament cannot be eliminated if the kerygma as a whole is to be preserved; but the mythology can be interpreted, and must be. The principle by which it is to be interpreted cannot, however, involve the elimination of wide areas of the content of the New Testament, as Bultmann's principle does. No principle of hermeneutics can be acceptable that precludes in advance anything being said about large areas of the literature to which it is applied. A principle more acceptable than Bultmann's would interpret the kerygma, including its mythological elements, in terms of its own intention. The results of the application of such a principle would depend, of course, on the presuppositions of the person who applied it. The understanding of the intention of the mythological elements will vary from interpreter to interpreter. But this

prior to modern times. Heaven and hell are understood
to be places like this earth, and to exist in some other
place, simultaneously with it. But they must not be so
understood. Neither heaven nor hell should be conceived
of as *places* created by God.

Heaven should be understood as where God is and we
are not. Of course, as soon as one says " where " he uses a
word connoting a place in space; but spatial language is
unavoidable because we have no other. Heaven means
that God is above and must come to us, for we cannot go
to him. He is raised and exalted, and we cannot reach
him; for God will indeed not " dwell on the earth "
(I Kings 8:27). Heaven, then, cannot be thought of as a
creation or created place, but only as where God is. It is
not created any more than God himself is created. To be
" in heaven " is to be where God is rather than separated
from him — to be reconciled to the Creator.

Hell is, conversely, where God is not. Whether conceived of as the place where the dead are, or as the place
of punishment, its meaning is that there man is separated
from God and therefore cannot live. Like heaven, it ought
not to be thought of as a created place, but is a mythological representation for the state of separation from the
source of life. Heaven and hell, then, are mythological
representations of metahistorical existence, either with or
without God. Or, to put it another way, they represent
life and death. Figuratively, they are used to represent life
and death, reconciliation and estrangement, in historical
existence.

2. *Jesus' Pre-existence.* Jesus' pre-existence is in no sense
a historical phenomenon. It concerns the prehistorical life
of the Savior which was never observable by historical
man. It is therefore a metahistorical myth whose meaning

for faith will be elaborated in Chapter X.

3. *Jesus' Descent Into Hades.* This expression does not occur in the New Testament, but the truth it points to is stated in I Peter 3:18 f. where Jesus is said to have gone " in the spirit " to preach to the " spirits in prison," and in ch. 4:6 of the same letter, where Christ is said to have preached also " to the dead " as well as to the living. The latter passage presupposes the former. What is alluded to in ch. 4:6 has already been described in ch. 3:19, although " the dead " in ch. 4:6 seem to include all who have died, whereas " the spirits in prison " in ch. 3:19 seem to refer specifically to the unrepentant in the time of Noah.[1]

Apparently, reference to Christ's descent, which later found its way into the Apostles' Creed, occurs in the New Testament only in I Peter. The passage in Ephesians (ch. 4:9) in which the author says that Jesus' ascension presupposes that he had " also descended into the lower parts of the earth," need not be taken and probably ought not to be taken as a reference to Jesus' descent into Hades. It should be understood rather in connection with Phil. 2:5 ff. where Jesus' descent from heaven to earth, and not from earth to Hades, is described.[2] It must be granted, however, that *ta katōtera merē tēs gēs* remains ambiguous.

But aside from the question of the number of places where Christ's descent into Hades is recorded, the belief that he descended is clearly implied in the New Testament, even though it belongs to the periphery of Christian teaching. Christ's descent is, of course, in no sense a historical event and is not described in the New Testament in terms that we have defined as historical. It is entirely metahistorical in character. What, then, is the meaning of this descent? It has two meanings. It refers, in the first place, to the final stage of Christ's self-emptying. Christ had been with God, and was God; but he emptied himself, was born as a man, humbled himself before Pilate and the world, and was crucified. This, however, was not his final self-humiliation; he also descended into the realm of the dead. That is to say, he *really* died, as every man must die, and his crucifixion was neither a mockery nor a fraud.

But Jesus' descent has a second meaning: it represents a part of his freeing act. As salvation comes through the gospel, and those who had died before Christ had descended to the prison of Hades without having heard the gospel, so Christ, at his death, opened up to those who had gone before him the possibility of life in his name. Hence the tombs were opened when Jesus yielded up his spirit (Matt. 27:52); in his hands were the keys of Death and of Hades (Rev. 1:18), and Christ tore away the power of death from the devil by destroying him (Heb. 2:14). Thus he has opened, for all, the way to eternal life. Christ is, himself, " the door of the Father through which enter in Abraham and Isaac and Jacob." [3]

4. *The Second Coming and the Last Judgment.* We consider these two together because they are so intimately related, for the judgment is to take place at the Second Coming: " from thence he shall *come* to *judge* the quick and the dead." These events, when described as yet to take place at the end of the age, are understood in the New Testament as historical; but they must be considered as myths of a purely metahistorical character which point to truths that are and will always be undemonstrable in any historical period. The truths to which the myths point are that Christ is the only judge and that he judges all. The *Last* Judgment points to the fact that no historical period follows the judgment — it is and always remains " last." It is also " last " in the sense of final, after which there is

no appeal. It is quite clear that whereas the Messiah has come, the Final Judgment which is in his hands has not yet been passed, but the judgment will be performed by him who alone is the criterion by which he judges. The norm of God's judgment is his will; and Christ as the Incarnate Word reveals this will to men. All who reject this will as revealed in Christ will be judged; and ultimately to reject Christ is ultimately to die.

HISTORICAL-METAHISTORICAL MYTHS

The second kind of myth in the New Testament consists of those which are partly historical and partly metahistorical. They point to events (or, in one case, *beings*) that occur in history — in the life of man — but also are related to the metahistorical realm in a way in which the historical myths are not. These myths are:

1. *Creation.* The myth of creation points both to God's eternal creation and to God's initial act as Creator. As the former it is in part historical, but as the latter it points to no specific historical moment. It is therefore both historical and metahistorical in character. It points to the faith that what is exists by virtue of a free will that caused what is, to be; and it attributes not only the present, but also the past and the future, the beginning and the end, to this same will. But the beginning and the end, the initial creation and the last things, are not to be thought of as occurring in the first and last periods of history. The myths of creation and of redemption (redemption being also creation) are metahistorical, although the former is also partly historical in that it refers not only to the first beginning, but to all new beginnings in history as well. Hence, it is both a metahistorical and a historical myth.

2. *Angels.* Angels are mythological beings which are de-

scribed in the New Testament as having both a historical and a metahistorical function. In the latter role they are the highest of created beings, serving God in heaven, in praise and adoration (Rev. 7:11 f.) ; as historical beings they implement his revelation and rule on earth. Angels ministered to Christ after his temptation (Matt. 4:11) ; an angel strengthened him on the Mount of Olives on the night on which he was betrayed (Luke 22:43) ; and an angel rolled back the stone from the entrance to Jesus' tomb after his burial (Matt. 28:2). Jesus, during his ministry, said that at the resurrection men would be like angels in heaven, neither marrying nor given in marriage (Mark 12:25) ; he spoke of the joy before the angels of God over one sinner who repents (Luke 15:10) ; and he said that at Lazarus' death he was carried by angels to Abraham's bosom (Luke 16:22). It was an angel who announced to Zechariah the birth of John the Baptist (Luke 1:11) ; and an angel told Joseph, in Matt. 1:20, and Mary, in Luke 1:26 (Gabriel), of the birth of Jesus. Angels frequently come to the assistance of the disciples in Acts (ch. 5:19, etc.) ; and Paul refers to them at eleven different places in his extant letters (not including Col. 2:18). In fact, angels are mentioned in eighteen of the twenty-seven New Testament writings.

The direct encounter of angels with men in historical existence seems to be described only in the Gospels and Acts; elsewhere the angels seem to be thought of as metahistorical in character. After the resurrection, however, the mediating function of angels in God's relation to the world was taken over by the Holy Spirit. As *historical* mythological beings, angels were to become superfluous. The confusion that existed in the early church between angels and the Holy Spirit is to be observed in the book of

The Acts. In Acts there seems to be no difference between angels, the Spirit, the Spirit of the Lord, and the Holy Spirit. Luke represents Paul as warned by the Holy Spirit (Acts 16:6), and then by the Spirit of Jesus (Acts 16:7), and later by an angel of God (Acts 27:23); and the authority of the first two seems not to be considered as any greater or more valid than the authority of the angel. Again, in the story of Philip and the Ethiopian eunuch, Philip is represented as being addressed first by an angel of the Lord (Acts 8:26) and then by the Spirit (Acts 8:29), and he obeys both as having equal or the same authority. No apparent distinction is made between them. In later canonical writings, however, the function of angels is confined to the metahistorical realm; but in the New Testament as a whole they are also considered as historical beings — that is, as entering into the flesh-and-blood existence of man.

3. *The Incarnation and the Virgin Birth.* We view these mythological representations together not because they are the same, or mean the same thing, but because for purposes of this classification they are very similar. They refer to the entrance of the Logos or Spirit into human history, in the person of Jesus. They therefore overlap the historical and the metahistorical, " coming " from the latter, as it were, into the former. The meaning of the virgin birth will be dealt with in the following chapter; the incarnation refers to God's having come to man in human form, to a unique entrance of God, himself, into human history, to Emmanuel — " God with us."

4. *The Resurrection.* This event and its meaning have been discussed in Chapter V and will be further elaborated in Chapter XII. It is mentioned here as belonging among the myths of this second group, as it is both historical and

metahistorical in character. It was an event that has been
" witnessed " in history and known, in faith, to have taken
place. But it also points to the victorious love of God
whose purposes death itself cannot defeat, and to the eternal life with God which is promised to those who love him.
This life, although it may be thought of as beginning in
history, is also promised for " posthistorical " existence. It
is in this sense metahistorical life; and the resurrection,
which points to Christ's metahistorical life as well as the
possibility of such life for believers, is to this extent a
metahistorical myth.

HISTORICAL MYTHS

We come now to the third kind or class of myth in the
New Testament. We have considered myths that point
to metahistorical truth, which describe " states " or
" places " or " events " that are in no sense historical. We
have noted myths that are partly of this type and partly
historical. But there are other myths in the New Testament that are there depicted and may be understood only
as having taken place or as yet to take place in history.
These are with more difficulty understood or recognized
as mythological, for they are also historical.

Before we look at these myths, let us first recall that we
have defined myths as dramatic stories in symbolic language, about God and his relation to men and the world,
which demand of man a decision and a commitment.[4] These
dramatic stories may be representations of events that
have occurred or are to occur in history. The New Testament records certain events that were historical in nature,
that were observable and describable by those who were
present to witness them, but which were later to be understood in faith as manifestations of the presence and

activity of God. The meanings of these events have been
different for faith than they have been apart from faith;
and in many cases the event itself has been so interpreted
in faith in the New Testament that a description of what
happened, apart from its meaning for faith, is no longer
recoverable. Such incidents are called mythological not
because they were not historical, but because as they are
narrated in the New Testament they are understood as
events in which God acted uniquely for man's salvation.
The New Testament record of these events does not pretend to be a scientific description of meaningless occurrences; it is rather a dramatic presentation of events that
are meaningful in faith (and that is the only reason they
have been recorded), in which God has been seen at work,
and which demand of man a decision or a commitment.
What are these events?

1. *Miracles.* The miracle stories in the Gospels are understandable only if their mythological character is presupposed. To refer to these stories as mythological, however, is not to imply that they are not historical. And to
affirm that many of them are so interpreted in faith that
their meaning apart from faith is no longer recoverable is
not, for that reason, to question their historicity. Jesus'
acts are never described in the Gospels except as they were
remembered by those who, since the acts had taken place,
had come to know him as their exalted Lord. There is no
story told of him that had not already been interpreted in
the light of the resurrection. But this is not to say that the
Gospel narratives are inaccurate and unhistorical; on the
contrary, it is to affirm that the meanings of the events as
they were recorded after the resurrection are more accurately given than would have been possible had the events
been recorded before the resurrection. This is true, how-

ever, only if God revealed himself in Christ; but if he did not, then the question of the accuracy or inaccuracy of the Gospel narratives is purely academic, and existentially and theologically irrelevant.

In other words, if the Gospel narratives are relevant to faith, the form in which we have them — already interpreted by faith — is the most accurate account of them we could have. The alternative to the interpretations given us would have been interpretations given in unbelief; but if Christ truly reveals God, then only an interpretation given in faith can be accurate. The only other possibility would have been to record the events without interpretation of any sort; but, again, if Christ manifests God, then such a record would have to be considered as made in unbelief and therefore in error. From the point of view of the church — of believers — the postresurrection interpretation of Jesus' life given in the Gospels must be considered as *truer,* i.e., as corresponding more closely to what God was saying and doing in Christ, than any preresurrection accounts of the events could have been. Whether or not this interpretation is true depends for its validation on the Parousia.

In conclusion we must add that clearly the miracles recorded in the Gospels are of various kinds, and each one should be treated separately. They ought not be lumped together as though they were all of one piece, for they are not. But the point we are now making is only that in varying degrees all the miracles have a mythological character.

2. *The Crucifixion.* The crucifixion is, so far as our classification of New Testament myths is concerned, unique in itself. But we have put it in this third group because it was an event within history in which God acted decisively. It was, of course, a historical event; but it was more than

that. There were thousands of crucifixions in the Roman Empire, but all of history is dated from only one. That crucifixion was not just a historical event; it was God's decisive act at the center of history. The language used to describe it as a divine act in history is, of necessity, mythological: there was darkness over the whole land (Mark 15:33) ; the light of the sun failed (Luke 23:45) ; the curtain of the Temple was torn in two from top to bottom (Mark 15:38) ; the earth shook, the rocks were split, and the tombs were opened (Matt. 27:51 f.) ; a heathen soldier identified the crucified One as a son of God (Mark 15:39) . This event broke the power of the devil (Heb. 2:14) , made expiation for man's sin to show that God, himself, is righteous (Rom. 3:25 f.) , revealed God's overpowering love for us (Rom. 5:8) , and secured an eternal redemption (Heb. 9:12) . All this and other language used to describe what happened that noon is mythological. It is dramatic and interpretive, communicating to those who will believe what God was doing there. The primary meanings that the New Testament accords to this event have been described and will be further analyzed in Chapter X. We are here concerned only to show that the crucifixion is both historical and mythological in character.

3. *The Antichrist.* The New Testament sometimes conceives of history as the locus of battle — the outcome of which is known, but the seriousness of which continues to be no less real — between Christ and his church and Satan and his cohorts. This hostility is expressed mythologically, but it is understood as historical in character, the opposition existing primarily on the plane of history. When God entered history in Christ, and Christ's Spirit founded the church, the forces of evil are depicted as rallying the more strenuously to overcome this unique incursion into the

domain of history where evil had thought itself in a position to be victorious. Therefore antidivine forces became specifically anti-Christian; for evil could not be victorious save it could conquer Christ, and to win out over God in Christ would be to win the final victory. The New Testament does not understand the event of Christ as leaving sin behind it. Sin is believed to have been overcome in principle; but Satan is yet to be crushed (Rom. 16:20), and the " lawless one " is yet to be slain (II Thess. 2:8).

The forces of evil are described, then, as working in the present, but also as concentrating all their energies for a final battle. They engage in persecution and oppression; but the last attack will be more subtle. At the end, evil will set itself up as good, the antichrist as Christ, the " lawless one " proclaiming himself to be God (II Thess. 2:4). The worst threat to faith is the possibility of mistaking evil for good, Satan for God; of allying oneself with the antichrist and so denying that Jesus is of God (I John 4:3).

The antichrist, then, is symbolic of all opposition to Christ and his church. He is " already at work " (II Thess. 2:7); but he is also the eschatological enemy who is preparing for the final deception against which the church must always be on guard in watching and in prayer. The antichrist is symbolic of the final degree of self-deification; he is the incarnation of evil posing as divine, and is symbolic of the fact that in no historical period is good not subject to attack.

4. *The Millennium.* A thousand years' reign of Christ with the martyrs and confessors of the church is portrayed in the Apocalypse, and only there. It is envisioned as taking place before Satan's final onslaught against the church, and as occurring while Satan is held bound in the bottom-

less pit. It is a mythological representation of the rule of Christ on earth. The length of this rule, a thousand years, is not to be understood literally, but as a very long time. The author of Revelation referred to heathen rule as lasting for three and a half years (Rev. 11:2; cf. 11:3; 12:6; 12:14; 13:5; also cf. Luke 21:24 and IV Ezra 5:4) ; but the rule of Christ is to be of far greater duration. Yet this rule will not mean the end of temptation, attack, and deceptions, for it will be followed by a new attack that only God himself will be able to defeat (Rev. 20:9-10; cf. II Thess. 2:3-8). This is the precarious position in which the church is always to exist — ever subject to a new attack greater than those of the past which, without the grace of God, would be disastrous. The church must always be watchful, if it think Satan be bound (cf. Mark 13:33-37) , lest he be loosed again and deceive the nations to gather them for battle. The growth of the church does not diminish the power of Satan. The millennium, then, is a mythological representation that concerns only historical existence.

5. *The Second Coming and the Holy Spirit.* The New Testament understands the Second Coming in two different ways: it understands it, in the first place, as an event that is always to take place in the future of any historical period, thereby indicating that every historical period stands under judgment — the purpose of the Second Coming being to judge. But the Second Coming is also understood in the New Testament as having already taken place, Christ having returned to his church in the Holy Spirit. Thus Jesus says: " I will come to you. Yet a little while, and the world will see me no more, but you will see me. . . ." (John 14:18-19) . " I go away, and I will come to you." (John 14:28.) John here apparently understands

this Second Coming of Jesus " in a little while " as the coming of the Paraclete or Holy Spirit, which Jesus promises to send his disciples (John 16:7) ; for here Jesus' statement " I will come to you " stands in the context of his promise of the Paraclete. As Bultmann writes of John 14:18: *eben im Kommen des Geistes kommt er selbst* (precisely in the coming of the Spirit does he [Jesus] himself come.) [5] And C. H. Dodd in his book on the Fourth Gospel points out that in John " Christ's coming again must be understood " partly in the sense that " the Paraclete will dwell " in the disciples.[6] For John the death and resurrection of Christ is radically eschatological in character. Thus the coming of the Holy Spirit is nothing else than the Second Coming of the Lord Christ. The Gospel of John is, however, not unambiguous in its identification of the Holy Spirit with the coming of Christ; for John does not relinquish the church's traditional eschatological expectation of a final fulfillment.

It should also be noted that in John the Paraclete is also the judge, as Christ is understood to be at his Second Advent. John says that when the Paraclete comes " he will convince the world of sin and of righteousness and of judgment " (John 16:8). Thus the Paraclete or Holy Spirit fulfills in John the function which, in other eschatological thought, Christ is to accomplish at his Second Coming. John thinks of Christ as having come to his church; and in this sense, the mythological event is thought of in historical terms. It is because Christ is in his church that Satan is moved to attack, and it is for the same reason that he will be defeated.

We have said that New Testament myths fall into one of three groups, and we have placed several of the major New Testament mythological elements in one of these categories. We believe that the value of such a classification is that it aids in discovering the meanings of the various myths. Since the contemporary view of history — as the plane on which men live out their lives — is quite different from the New Testament view that understands all the events to which it refers as historical, we believe it is helpful to apply the contemporary view as to what may rightly be considered history, and what may not, to the various events all of which in the New Testament are represented as historical.

Although such a classification aids, in this respect, in understanding New Testament myths, we are also aware that it breaks up and confuses the New Testament kerygma to the point where a proper perspective on the whole of what is said is lost. To compensate for this confusion, let us rearrange in their proper order the myths we have just disarranged, keeping in mind the classification we have discussed. It will be seen that the myths refer at first to metahistorical events, then to historical events, and finally to metahistorical events again, with myths that are partly both, in between.

The creation of the world by God, and of everything that exists, including heaven and hell, is presupposed in the New Testament. Angels, the highest beings that he has made, surround the throne and sing the praises of the Almighty, the King of creation. With God was his Word, and the Word was God. This Word was incarnate by the Holy Spirit of the Virgin Mary and was made man. In the Word made flesh — Jesus of Nazareth, who was the Christ — God entered uniquely and decisively into history for man's salvation. Christ manifested the power and love of God for all who would see, in his miracles as well as in other ways. But he was crucified, and, as he was a man, he died. He descended, then, to Hades. There he preached to the spirits in prison, and set free those who had preceded him in history. On the third day, God raised him from the dead. Christ then returned to his disciples and re-established the relationship that death for a short time had broken. His Spirit founded the church — the community of sinners who are redeemed. But the power of evil rallied in opposition to the presence of Christ in his church. This opposition continues throughout all succeeding historical periods. Christ reigns for a long time, but the powers of evil remain free to attack. All men of all historical time stand under the judgment of Christ; but to those who believe, the Kingdom is given, and such things as pass man's understanding are promised the faithful.

This is the barest outline of the gospel, which the New Testament proclaims in mythological language. The chief elements in it are the incarnation — the breaking into history of the Word made flesh, and the crucifixion-resurrection which seals the meaning of the incarnation. The mythological language that describes these events is the center and kernel of the kerygma. All other myths derive their meaning and significance from these two primary events. But each myth is a part of the story and has its place in the saga of God's dealing with mankind through Christ.

VIII

Eschatology

BULTMANN'S VIEW

We must consider one final implication of Bultmann's demythologization. It is the subject of eschatology. For Bultmann, the eschatological event has already taken place, and is now occurring; it is not still to happen in the future. Significant quotations from his " Neues Testament und Mythologie " follow:

The crucifixion is " the eschatological event; that is, it is not an event of the past to which one looks back, but it is the eschatological event in time and beyond time in so far as its meaning is understood in faith as always present." [1] Bultmann elaborates his point by referring to Paul's statement that in baptism one is baptized into the death of Christ (Rom. 6:3) and is crucified with him (Rom. 6:6). In the Lord's Supper the Christian proclaims the death of Christ (I Cor. 11:26), and the cup and the bread are participations in the body of Christ (I Cor. 10:16). " The cross of Christ is always present in the concrete life of the believer "; [2] " those who belong to Christ Jesus have crucified the flesh . . ." (Gal. 5:24). And so Paul says that in the cross of the Lord Jesus Christ, the world has been crucified to him and he to the world (Gal. 6:14); and he writes to the Philippians that he has suffered partly in order to share Christ's sufferings and become like him in his death (Phil. 3:8-10; cf. II Cor. 4:10 f.) .

Furthermore, the cross and resurrection are for Bultmann a " cosmic unity " and the resurrection is also " an eschatological event." [3] He writes, " It is clear that throughout the New Testament the resurrection of Christ is the eschatological event." [4] Or again: " In the proclamation of the Word, cross and resurrection become present and the eschatological Now takes place. The eschatological promise of Isa. 49:8 is fulfilled: ' Behold, now is the acceptable time; behold, now is the day of salvation.' " [5] And so is brought about " the resurrection life in the believers." [6] Bultmann then quotes John 5:24 f. in which eternal life is described as present for whoever hears and believes; and the judgment is already passed on him who does not believe (John 9:39; 12:31). And finally, both the Word and the church are said to belong to " the eschatological event." [7]

These quotations are sufficient to reveal the fact that Bultmann understands the whole Christ event — the crucifixion, the resurrection, the preaching of the Word, and the church — as having occurred at the end of history, and not at its mid-point. Bultmann's elaboration of New Testament eschatology includes nothing that does not take place now, in the present time. For him the *present* is the end-time; the Parousia has taken place, Christ being present in the preached Word; and the judgment to life or death occurs at the hearing of the Word. Bultmann has thus demythologized the doctrines of the Second Coming and of the Last Judgment; and he says nothing about the millennium or the *final* resurrection, as he believes these cannot be demythologized. He is consistent here in demythologizing what he can, in interpreting existentially what he believes to be the timeless relevance of eschatological events, and in eliminating the rest.

KÜMMEL'S CRITICISM

Bultmann's handling of New Testament eschatology has
been rather strongly attacked. Kümmel argues that the
early church definitely expected a *future* Parousia, that
Paul also awaited a fulfillment of the new age which had
begun,[8] and that even John, whom Bultmann frequently
quotes to support his understanding of "present eschatology," "contains future eschatological tensions." [9] Kümmel, however, is also willing to make distinctions among
the several apocalyptic views of eschatological events. He
states, for example, that the millennium is not in continuity with the central New Testament kerygma. Although, then, he insists on the future aspect of the eschaton, he, along with Bultmann, would eliminate what he
considers to be peripheral — and perhaps even erroneous
— details of the eschatological events described in the New
Testament.

VIEWS OF ALTHAUS AND SCHNIEWIND

Representing a more conservative point of view is Paul
Althaus, who writes that " the gospel preaches not only a
present salvation but also promises a future salvation as
well." [10] Althaus emphasizes that we ought not speak
simply of individual salvation, but that we ought to stress
" the universal hope for the Kingdom of God coming at
the end of history," [11] which hope has been virtually given
up in many theological quarters and not by Bultmann
alone. Althaus continues that science cannot speak of an
end of world history or of the cosmos; only faith can speak
of such an end. And faith must so speak because it cannot

believe in an endless opposition of God and the world.[12] " The end of history and of the world is the Parousia of Christ." [13] And at this Parousia the whole world will be judged: " The judgment of God will not be merely personal and private, but it will be a public and common experience in which all mankind will participate. We shall stand with one another, in a common guilt, before the judgment of God." [14] But before the judgment must come the antichrist — one who puts himself in the place of Christ. The Christian must always know that trials and temptations are ever a possibility until the end of history, and for these he must prepare in watching and praying. This, says Althaus, " is the meaning for us of the early Christian expectation " of the antichrist.[15] And finally, the end comes.

The Second Coming of Christ brings with it the fulfillment of history, the Kingdom of God. " The Kingdom of God is not supraworldly, standing over earthly history, but is history's aim. History cannot bring forth the Kingdom out of itself; but it lies in travail . . . until the Kingdom should come." [16] Althaus believes that the new world — the Kingdom of God — will follow immediately upon the end of history and he, too, rejects the idea of an intermediate thousand years' reign of Christ. Thus Althaus preserves and interprets literally all the eschatological details found in the New Testament except the millennium.

Schniewind also writes against Bultmann that, in the New Testament, eschatology is " end-history " — that is, " end " from the point in time of present history; and he adds that science is not in a position to say that there will be no such end.[17] Thus, according to Althaus, science cannot speak of the end of world history; and according to Schniewind, science cannot deny such an end.

The main objection raised against Bultmann is not that he does not make room for all the eschatological material in the New Testament, such as the millennium which the far more conservative Althaus also rejects, but that he transmutes eschatological expectations into present realities. For Bultmann, the *eschata* — the last things — are here, now; and the church ought not look for or promise any " last things " along the horizontal line of history that are different from what exists in the present. Bultmann will thus not speak of an " end " or culmination of history; every moment is equidistant from the end, as Leopold von Ranke believed.[18]

ESCHATOLOGY IN TILLICH, BERDYAEV, AND REINHOLD NIEBUHR

Tillich's philosophy of history and eschatology bears a resemblance in one respect to Bultmann's, for Tillich also interprets Christian eschatology entirely in nontemporal terms. For him, as for Bultmann, it is inconceivable that the eschatological events pictured in the New Testament should happen at the end of history. He writes that although history must be thought of as having a beginning and an end, " neither the end nor the beginning of history can be designated on the plane of physical time." [19] They must be interpreted symbolically. It is here that Tillich differs from Bultmann: he will interpret symbolically what Bultmann will not interpret at all because of his inability to demythologize; and this is a significant difference. Thus Tillich writes that " the doctrine of the millennium should not be interpreted as a static final condition, and certainly not in Augustine's sense of the sovereignty of the hierarchy." [20] In this Bultmann would agree. But then Tillich goes on to interpret the millennium as

" the symbol of the victory over concrete demonic forces within history." [21] Tillich thus gives meaning to a doctrine that Bultmann eliminates, although Tillich rejects all literal interpretations of last events, including the Kingdom of God: " To expect that . . . in some future age the demonic as a whole will be utterly destroyed is a religious ' utopianism ' which should be regarded as quite untenable." [22] Tillich removes the *eschaton* from the end of history and locates it " above " history whence it impinges on the course of human life.

Berdyaev, more than Tillich, tries to give a future meaning to eschatological events; [23] but it must be said that his emphasis remains on their present reality. His attempt to hold the two meanings together is well shown in his statement: " The paradox of eschatological consciousness is that the end is both put off to an indefinite time in the future and is near to every moment of life." [24] But Berdyaev elaborates the latter meaning far more than the former, as he shows when he continues:

> There is an eschatology within the process of life. Apocalypse is not merely the revelation of the end of the world and of history. It is also the revelation of the end within the world and the historical process, within human life and every moment of life.[25]

And in *The Meaning of History* he writes, " Exoterically the Apocalypse is simply the expression in convenient symbols of the esoteric apocalypse of the human spirit." [26]

Reinhold Niebuhr also interprets eschatological events in terms of their present meaning, but he tries as well to maintain their final or " end " meaning.[27] He writes that:

> Eternity stands over time on the one hand and at the end of time on the other. It stands over time in the sense that it is the ultimate source and power of all derived

and dependent existence. . . . Eternity stands at the end
of time in the sense that the temporal process cannot be
conceived without a *finis;* and eternity cannot be conceived as having a *finis.*[28]

He accepts von Ranke's statement that " each moment of
time and history is equidistant from eternity," but adds
that " history is also a total process which requires understanding of its totality from some ' last judgment.' " [29]
Niebuhr, then, interprets the various " last things " in
terms of their present and final meanings. For example, of
the Parousia he writes:

> This return of Christ stands at the " end " of history in
> such a way that it would sometimes appear to be a tri-
> umph in history and to mean a redeemed temporal-
> historical process. . . . And the redemption of history
> would appear to be its culmination also. This twofold
> aspect of the final vindication of Christ implies a refuta-
> tion in Biblical faith of both utopianism and a too con-
> sistent otherworldliness.[30]

In other words, Niebuhr will not give up his faith in either
present meanings and fulfillments within history, or in a
final meaning and culmination of the historical process
under the sovereignty of God. To believe in the former
alone is to be " otherworldly "; to believe in the latter
alone is to be " utopian."

I find it impossible, however, to understand how Niebuhr can say that the temporal process cannot be conceived without a *finis,* eternity standing " at the end of
time," and still accept von Ranke's dictum that each moment of time is equidistant from eternity. If eternity
stands at the *end* of time, how can each moment of time
be equidistant from eternity? History does " move," and
if each moment of time is equidistant from eternity, and

eternity stands at the " end " of time, then the meaning of " end " must be redefined, or another word might better be used.

The same apparent contradiction is to be found in *Beyond Tragedy* where Niebuhr says that " the realm of fulfillment is at the end of history " but " the end of history is not a point in history "; [31] and, " we do not believe that the human enterprise will have a tragic conclusion." [32] Must not the conclusion of the human enterprise refer to a point in history? (It can hardly refer to a point *outside* of history.) And if it must, then Niebuhr is affirming God's victory at a point in history — namely, its end. But the point remains obscure. Niebuhr does not want to be found guilty of defending a too simple religious utopianism, and yet he wishes to hold on to the Biblical faith in a culmination of history. He seems unwilling to relinquish his faith in a final consummation — final, in the temporal sense — although his use of the word " end " and of the phrase " point in history " is not clear.

I have raised this question concerning Dr. Niebuhr's interpretation because it would appear that, although not clearly, he does justice to the tension found in the New Testament between future hope and present reality. Paul " presses forward " (Phil. 3:12 ff.) although he agrees that *now* is " the day of salvation " (II Cor. 6:2) ; in John the judgment has already taken place in the presence of Christ — the light in the darkness (John 12:31) , and it is yet to take place " on the last day " (John 12:48) ; in the Apocalypse, Jesus stands at the door and knocks (Rev. 3:20) , but the Apocalypse closes with the prayer that he will come (Rev. 22:20) . And throughout the New Testament there is the tension between present and future judgment, between the presence of Christ in his church and the hope

for his coming, between the awareness of being a new creation and the expectation of a new life with Christ, between the consciousness of being raised with Christ and
the hope for the resurrection. If justice is to be done to
New Testament eschatology, this tension between what is
and what will be, between the end as having come and the
end as yet to come, must be maintained. The tension is
illustrated by two passages in the New Testament in which
the Greek word *synteleia* (end) is used. In Hebrews 9:26
Jesus is said to have appeared already " once for all at the
end [*synteleia*] of the age "; and in Matthew 28:20 Jesus
promises to be with his disciples *until* the " end [*synteleia*]
of the age " — yet to come.

CRITICISM AND DEFENSE OF BULTMANN

Bultmann's understanding of eschatology is only half
true, or perhaps one might say three quarters true. For
Bultmann does not give up the tension between present
and future. The tension that he understands, however, is
one between my present and the next moment of my future, rather than between my (or, our) present and my
(or, our) ultimate future. But if we are to do justice to the
New Testament's understanding of the community and of
history, we must not narrow the eschatological tension so
that its meaning is confined to personal life, and does not
also include the larger community of the household of
faith and the history of the world as well.

Bultmann, I think, is quite right in his understanding
that the individual believer lives in his own private tension between what is now and what shall be. Paul speaks
out of his personal experience when he writes that " since
we are justified by faith, we have peace with God " — *now*
(Rom. 5:1) ; and he adds quite confidently that since we

have been justified by his blood, "much more shall we be saved by him from the wrath of God " (Rom. 5:9). And yet Paul also knows that he must one day face a judge and stand before an unknown future (II Cor. 5:10). And every believer lives within the eschatological tension of his own present and his own future; the future is in a sense present and in a sense not yet. Every believer is judged and will be judged, is raised and hopes for the resurrection, knows Christ in the church and looks for his coming, believes that in the resurrection God was victorious over the powers of evil, and yet knows too well that these powers have not yet been laid low.

But the New Testament speaks not only to man as an individual but also to man as a member of a community, and as one creature who exists for a short time in a long historical process. And man asks not only about himself but also about his community and his world, to which he knows he is in some sense inextricably bound and without which his own life is meaningless. Personal salvation is not divorceable from social salvation; indeed, the former depends on the possibility of the latter. A god who is only my lord and is not Lord of all cannot save one human soul. One ought not think in spatial terms of a province for God and a province for Satan, and rest his hope for salvation on being snatched over the border into God's domain; and even if one does so think, God's province would always be subject to attack and perhaps to defeat. This is the meaning of the final battle between the forces of good and the forces of evil portrayed apocalyptically in the book of Revelation. It points to the genuineness of salvation, to God's final and ultimate Lordship over the world, in the context of which alone salvation is possible. And so the Christian faith looks for a consummation, and the Christian believes

that God will, in his own time, take up his great power
and rule, that he will finally destroy the powers of evil,
that the inequalities and injustices of life and of history
will be rectified, that hidden meanings will be revealed,
and that the things that God has prepared for those who
love him will be manifest.

I do not quite see the significance of Dr. Niebuhr's
statement that time cannot be thought of without a *finis*,
for I cannot conceive of time as *having* a *finis* any more
easily than I can conceive of it as *not* having one. What
would the end of time be like? I do not see, therefore,
that one's inability to conceive of time as not having an
end is a convincing argument for the necessity of there
being such an end. Faith, alone, postulates an end, and it
would appear that the " end " like the " beginning " must
remain shrouded in mystery. The myth of Creation points
to the belief that what is exists by virtue of a free Will and
not because of an immutable law of cause and effect in
which only one " effect " is possible in each new situation.

So eschatology points to the belief that the future will
exist by virtue of the same free Will which brought into
being what is. The end, like the beginning, will not be
accidental or the result of pure chance, but will be caused
by the same Will that caused the beginning. The meaning that the doctrine of Creation ascribes to the beginning,
and to every new emergence in history, is ascribed in eschatology to the end; and eschatology points to no particular time in the future (" Of that day or that hour no one
knows. . . ." Mark 13:32) as the doctrine of Creation
points to no specific time in the past.

I agree with Bultmann to the extent that the New Testament understands the final, eschatological events as im-
pinging in the present on the lives of believers, and that

in this sense eschatological events are present reality. But I also believe that the last things of which the New Testament speaks are interpreted there, and must be interpreted by us, as also referring to events that are yet to take place in a final way to be distinguished from their provisional manifestations in the present. To say that Christ instituted the final era before the consummation, that the Christ-event was and is the eschatological event, that the church and the preaching of the Word belong to this event, and that believers live in the " eschatological Now," must not lead to an affirmation — explicit or implicit — that all that is now is all that ever shall be. Such a view cannot be either derived from or harmonized with the New Testament.

Although we must affirm that the New Testament proclaims a consummation of the present and denies that the *last* things have already taken place in a final way, we must also affirm that one cannot look to any point within the historical process itself for the consummation of history. The doctrine of the Second Coming includes belief in a final consummation, but it must not be interpreted as a historical event. It points to the vindication of the righteous, but one must not be led to expect that the righteous will necessarily be vindicated in history: *superna est enim sanctorum civitas.*[33] This is precisely the meaning of the Last Judgment — that injustices and moral ambiguities will remain in history to the very end.

PART THREE

A Reinterpretation of Eschatology, Jesus' Pre-existence and Virgin Birth, His Crucifixion and Resurrection

IX

New Testament Eschatology

THE "END" AS HAVING COME

When one reads the New Testament one gains the strong impression that the authors believed that they were writing about and under the impact of the decisive event in history. To understand the origin of this belief one must try to understand what the records bequeath concerning Jesus' life and work.

Jesus began his ministry, according to our earliest Gospel, with the words, " The time is fulfilled, and the kingdom of God is at hand; repent, and believe in the gospel " (Mark 1:15). Jesus believed that the Kingdom was " at hand," or had " come near." More than that, he believed that in his own work the powers of the Kingdom were already being unleashed. He said, " If it is by the finger of God that I cast out demons, then the kingdom of God has come upon you." (Luke 11:20; Matt. 12:28.) When the Baptist sent his disciples to ask Jesus, " Are you he who is to come, or shall we look for another? " Jesus told them to go back and tell John what they had seen and heard — the Messianic expectations were being fulfilled in him (Matt. 11:2-6 and Luke 7:18-23). Jesus said on another occasion that the Kingdom of heaven had suffered violence from the days of John the Baptist until now (Matt. 11:12), implying that the Kingdom was not simply future, but that in some way it had already come. And again, " Whoever does not receive the kingdom of God like a child shall not enter it " [1] implies that it is available now or in the future, to be received by those who are childlike.

And there are many other passages in the Synoptic Gospels that reflect the same belief — that the Kingdom had drawn near and that in a new, special, and decisive way God's rule was being inaugurated in history. Frequently, words attributed in the Gospels to the historical Jesus actually had their origin at a slightly later period; but that Jesus preached the imminence of the Kingdom, and that he believed that God was acting in a unique way toward the establishment of the Kingdom is, I think, unquestionable.

There is another factor recorded in the Gospels that points to the early church's belief that in Christ the Messianic age had dawned, and that is the appearance of the Holy Spirit. There was an expectation in Judaism that the Spirit would accompany the Messiah and would be poured out at his Advent. Several Old Testament passages were used to support this belief,[2] and later Jewish writings, especially of the first century before Christ, elaborate the expectation.[3]

In the Old Testament the spirit of God is active at the Creation, brooding upon the face of the waters; so also in the New Testament is the Spirit active in the creation of the new age. The introduction of the Spirit in the infancy narratives of both Matthew and Luke points to the Messianic and eschatological character of the birth of Christ. Gabriel's words to Mary, " The Holy Spirit will come upon you, and the power of the Most High will overshadow you " (Luke 1:35) are probably a reminiscence of

Gen. 1:2. The Spirit, which was present at the foundation
of the world, which had not been seen since the days of
the prophets, and which was to reappear at the end of the
age, does appear and brings to pass the birth of the Messiah, the inaugurator of the age to come.

This same Spirit reappears at the baptism of the Messiah, who is at that time personally endowed with the
Spirit that was to be given at the end of the age. As Bultmann says of Jesus' baptism:

> One ought not to speak psychologically of the narrative
> of a call, or even designate its content as a call given
> through a vision. It is to be distinguished from all ac-
> counts of calls. . . . It is the account . . . of (Jesus)
> becoming Messiah and Son of God, which cannot be de-
> scribed as a call. . . . The legend reports Jesus' inaugu-
> ration to Messiahship, and is therefore basically not a
> biographical legend but a legend of faith.[4]

Moving on, we note that in the account of Jesus' temptation, the only thing other than that Jesus was tempted,
which is common to all three Synoptic Gospels, is that it
was the Spirit who drove Jesus to confront the tempter.
This temptation expresses mythologically the conflict with
cosmic implications, between the Messiah and the powers
of evil. As Montefiore says, " Both in Mark and in Q the
temptation is ' Messianic ': i.e., it is the temptation of the
Messiah, not of an ordinary individual." [5] In this conflict
the devil is defeated, but he is not destroyed. Thus at the
beginning of Jesus' ministry, his Messiahship is both affirmed and represented as being secret.[6] The destruction
of Satan would have been a visible manifestation of Messiahship; but the Messiah defeats Satan silently and invis-
ibly, in an isolated spot, and allows him a limited future.

Jesus' Messiahship is from that moment, throughout his whole earthly life, hidden. Only supernatural beings, or men enlightened from the supernatural realm, identify him correctly. But *that* Jesus was the Messiah is already implied when Mary is described as " with child of the Holy Spirit " (Matt. 1:18).

Jesus' Messiahship as hidden and revealed continues in his later confrontation with evil spirits, which he was able to exorcise. Just how common exorcisms were in Palestine in the time of Jesus it is difficult to say. The Old Testament scarcely contains a parallel to those of Jesus, the closest thing to them being the story of David's harp-playing which leads to the departure of an evil spirit from Saul (I Sam. 16:14-23). Exorcisms are equally scarce in the Apocrypha and pseudepigrapha, the one such case in the Apocrypha being in the book of Tobit (chs. 6:4 to 8:3). But this story is of such a magical character that perhaps it ought not be considered as a case of exorcism at all.[7]

In Rabbinical literature, however, there are many references to demons, and to their being exorcised from men. Strack and Billerbeck cite examples of this.[8] However, Israel Abrahams has observed that the great amount of demonology found in the Babylonian Talmud cannot be cited as applicable to the time of Jesus in the Holy Land. It is no wonder, he maintains, that the Pharisees were amazed at Jesus' exorcisms.[9] If, however, the Q saying of Jesus, addressed to the Jews in Luke and to the Pharisees in Matthew, " If I cast out demons by Beelzebul, by whom do your sons cast them out? " is authentic, then Jesus cannot have been the only Jewish exorcist in the Palestine of his day (Matt. 12:27 and Luke 11:19).

The difficulty nevertheless remains that no exorcisms other than those which Jesus performed are definitely

known to have taken place in Palestine during the life of
Jesus. My former teacher, Dr. S. Vernon McCasland, in a
very thorough study of demon possession and exorcism in
early Christianity, is quite convinced that exorcisms were
" well known in the Palestine of his [Jesus'] day." [10] But
he offers no proof of this — only a deduction that could
possibly be warranted, but that need not be. He refers to
the two cases we have mentioned — the exorcism of the
evil spirit from Saul by David, and the questionable exorcism recorded in the book of Tobit; and then Dr. McCasland assumes that:

> It is natural to infer that, as demonology assumed in-
> creasingly more importance in Jewish theology, exorcism
> continued, so that there is no break in continuity be-
> tween the early exorcists who used a lyre [11] and those of
> the Gospels.

But is this a natural inference in the light of such silence?
Jewish literature does reflect an increase in demonology,
but it does not reflect a corresponding increase in exorcism; and such an increase is not necessarily to be deduced.
Dr. McCasland cites only two other cases of Jewish exorcism that would be relevant to first-century Palestine: one
from the Book of Jubilees [12] which does not refer to exorcism of the mentally deranged but to various medicines
with which to heal; the second from Josephus' *Antiquities* [13] which was written in Rome after A.D. 70, and is
laden with obviously legendary material. And so the question of how prevalent exorcisms were in the Palestine of
Jesus' day remains unanswerable.

So far as exorcisms among the Greeks and Romans of
the first century are concerned, Dr. McCasland concludes
that exorcisms may have been performed among them,

" but there is very slight evidence of them." [14] Moreover,
" there is not a single authentic Greek or Roman document of the first century, except the New Testament,
which shows a case of demon possession and exorcism." [15]
I know of no evidence to refute this.

But regardless of the commonness or uncommonness of
exorcisms in Palestine and in the Hellenistic world of the
first century, it is quite clear that Jesus' exorcisms were regarded in the church as unique in that they were signs of
the Kingdom of God. Exorcisms in the New Testament
are Messianic and eschatological in character.[16] Exorcism
was apparently not usually thought of in Judaism as a
function of the Messiah, but the church understood Jesus'
exorcisms as manifestations of his Messianic power. They
were a sign of the fact that the Messiah had come and that
his power was being exerted. They were regarded as visible manifestations of the victory that Jesus had won in
principle at his temptation — visible, however, only to
supernatural beings. And as in the case of Jesus' victory at
his temptation, so with his exorcisms: they were believed
in the church to have had cosmic significance.

In Mark 3:27, Jesus says, " No one can enter a strong
man's house and plunder his goods, unless he first binds
the strong man; then indeed he may plunder his house."
And in Matthew 12:28 Jesus says, " If it is by the Spirit of
God that I cast out demons, then the kingdom of God has
come upon you." In Mark, Jesus has said (ch. 3:23-26)
that Satan is clearly active; hence he is not divided. Nevertheless, Satan's kingdom is falling under the attack of the
outsider. Who is this outsider? It can be only God or his
Messiah. And in Matthew, Jesus denies that he casts out
demons by the prince of demons and says that he exorcises
by the power of God. And when he so acts, the powers of

the Kingdom are made manifest. It is well known that the exact meaning of *ephthasen* is difficult to determine; but regardless of its precise meaning, Jesus here intimately relates his exorcisms to the presence of the Kingdom. As Barrett says in an excellent book, Jesus' exorcisms " are not magic or thaumaturgy; they are not occasional miracles granted in answer to the prayer of a sage or holy man; they are a particular and unique event in God's fulfillment of his promise of redemption in his Kingdom." [17]

Finally, Jesus' crucifixion is understood in the New Testament as a conflict between the Messiah and the power of God, on the one hand, and the evil spirits of the cosmos, on the other. The New Testament does not often interpret the crucifixion as a struggle between Christ and the devil (some later theologians make much more of this than the New Testament does) ; but the interpretation, though uncommon, is nevertheless present. Paul in one passage (I Cor. 2:8) lays the blame for the crucifixion on " the rulers of this age " — by which designation he undoubtedly includes supernatural evil spirits (cf. I Cor. 15:24; Rom. 16:20) ; and the author of Hebrews says that Christ became man that " through death he might destroy . . . the devil " (Heb. 2:14) .

But Jesus' death is seen even more clearly in the Gospels than elsewhere in the New Testament as the culmination of a struggle of cosmic proportions between Christ and the powers of evil that issues in the final, decisive victory of God's Messiah. Note the strange words that Luke records Jesus as having said to those who captured him in Gethsemane, " This is your hour, and the power of darkness " (Luke 22:53) . They seem to mean that human sin and the powers of evil are here combined against the Lord's Anointed. But the resurrection is the only proof the dis-

ciples needed as to who won that battle. In Peter's first
speech in Acts (ch. 2:22-36) the *whole* of the emphasis is
on what God *has* done in Christ: "This Jesus . . . you
crucified and killed. . . . But God raised him up." Then
the Sixteenth Psalm is quoted as prophecy of the resurrection. Christ "was not abandoned to Hades. . . . This
Jesus God raised up, and of that we are all witnesses." And
"he has poured out this which you see and hear" — the
Holy Spirit. "Let all the house of Israel . . . know as-
suredly that God has made him both Lord and Christ."
There is not a mention of a Second Coming of this Jesus
who has been made both Lord and Christ; nor is there even
an allusion to any further, future vindication of victory.
And the Latin hymn captures the same spirit when it says,
"The strife is o'er, the battle done; the victory of life is
won."

It is also interesting to observe that in not one of
Jesus' resurrection appearances in any of the Gospels does
he speak of a future event that will vouchsafe the past.
How anticlimactic would any such statement be at the end
of the gospel story!

We must also note the Gospels' description of the clos-
ing hours of Jesus' life. During the last three hours "there
was darkness over the whole land" (Mark 15:33 and parallels) ; and when Jesus breathed his last "the curtain of the
Temple was torn in two" (Luke 23:45; Matt. 27:51), and
Matthew adds that "the earth shook, and the rocks were
split; and the tombs were opened" (Matt. 27:51 f.). Aside
from certain precise meanings of these words, it is clear
that what took place then was understood as having cosmic
significance, the sign of Satan's defeat being observable in
the world of space and time. The Messiah was victorious;
his age had come; God's power was now being decisively

and in a final way employed.[18]

This emphasis found in the Synoptic Gospels on what God did in Christ, this belief that the Messianic age, so long hoped for, had come, is equally characteristic of the rest of the New Testament. It is clear that the Johannine writings stress the *fulfillment* of Messianic expectations in Christ. Indeed, Bultmann holds that the original, unredacted Johannine view was that no future consummation or validation was to be expected. Even the Last Judgment is now taking place. One who believes will not be further judged, for he has already passed from death to eternal life (John 5:24) ; and the Second Coming has already taken place in the coming of the Holy Spirit.[19]

Paul also speaks of those who are perishing now, and of those who are now being saved (II Cor. 2:15; 4:3 f.) . He believes that Christians *are* a new creation (II Cor. 5:17) , that they have been brought from death to life (Rom. 6:13) , and have been delivered from the dominion of darkness (Col. 1:13) ; that they have *now* received reconciliation (Rom. 5:11) , that there is for them now no condemnation (Rom. 8:1) , that Christians have been made alive with Christ and raised up with him and made to sit with him in the heavenly places (Eph. 2:5-8) , for the end of the ages has come (I Cor. 10:11) , and now is the day of salvation (II Cor. 6:2) . He is consumed by what God has done in Christ and he sings lyrically of the bonds that have been broken and of the life that has been given; for death, man's last enemy, has been swallowed up in victory. " Thanks be to God who gives us — yes, *is giving* us (*didonti*) — the victory through our Lord Jesus Christ " (I Cor. 15:53, 57) .

Non-Pauline epistles make the same point again and again. A few quotations will illustrate:

" Take hold of the eternal life to which you were called."
(I Tim. 6:12.)

" Baptism . . . now saves you." (I Peter 3:21.)

" God . . . saved us." (II Tim. 1:9.)

" The grace of God has appeared for the salvation of all
men." (Titus 2:11.)

" Let us be grateful for receiving a kingdom that cannot
be shaken." (Heb. 12:28.)

That the Messiah has come, every book of the New Testament explicitly testifies, except one. The exception is
III John, which never refers to Christ in any way, but
speaks three times of the church, which presupposes Christ.
The Kingdom and the life that God gives in the Kingdom
are now available. The decisive event in history is no
longer to be expected or to be hoped for; it has already
taken place. " Behold, *now* is the acceptable time; behold,
now is the day of salvation " (II Cor. 6:2) .

The " End " as Yet to Come

But the New Testament speaks not only of what has happened in the past, and of what is taking place in the present; it also looks forward to a fulfillment in the future, to
a consummation of what has been begun. It is at this point
that Professor Bultmann's interpretation of New Testament eschatology meets, it seems to me, insuperable diffi-
culties. For although Christ saw Satan fall like lightning
from heaven (Luke 10:18) , Paul much later knew that
Satan was still at work on the earth (I Cor. 7:5; II Cor.
2:11, etc.) . On the one hand, the victory was won; but on
the other hand, the battle was still raging. We must now
examine a few passages in the New Testament that look to
the future for fulfillment, and then seek to determine in

what sense the New Testament message as a whole can be understood.

It is widely recognized today that Jesus' teachings were largely eschatological in character. Since the publication, in 1892, of Johannes Weiss's *The Preaching of Jesus About the Kingdom of God,* scholars who on other questions represent different points of view have more and more realized that Jesus taught under the impact of his expectation that God was about to take up his great power and rule.[20] The signs of the times were clear, the powers of the Kingdom were already at work; man must repent and believe in the gospel. Jesus knew that the time was fulfilled, that the Kingdom of God was at hand, and that it was urgent for men to repent immediately and to believe in the gospel. All his teaching presupposes this assumption of what God had already done and was doing, and his belief in the necessity of an immediate acceptance of God's action by men.

The negative deduction, which is sometimes drawn, that because Jesus preached the urgency of repentance and belief he did not believe that history as we know it would be prolonged except for a few months or years, may be unwarranted, but in any case is irrelevant except for the historian. The kerygma is not affected by whether or not Jesus may have been in error concerning the time when future events would occur. The content of the gospel is what God has done in Christ, and not Jesus' foreknowledge. Any error discovered in the realm of the latter would be quite irrelevant to the church's belief in and proclamation of the Lordship of Christ. Jesus is the truth, not in the sense that he communicates scientific knowledge or predicts the dates of future events, but only in the sense that he communicates knowledge needed for salvation, which knowledge is given, finally, only in him.

We have said that Jesus refers to a future fulfillment as
well as to a present reality. Or, as it might be put more exactly, Jesus preaches that the Kingdom is at hand, urges
acceptance of it, and refers to the difficulty of entering it
and to the awful consequences of rejecting it. It is, however, highly questionable that Jesus elaborated in any detail on when the Kingdom would be fulfilled, or on the
nature of the Kingdom as fulfilled. The early church spoke
much more about the *future* Kingdom than Jesus did; it
therefore reinterpreted many of Jesus' sayings and parables
as referring to the Parousia, the Last Judgment, and the
Kingdom. Let us look at two such cases.

First, the parable of the talents, as it is in Matthew, or
the pounds, in Luke (Matt. 25:14-30; Luke 19:12-27).
Whether this parable was derived from Q or whether Matthew and Luke knew it in quite different forms is imma-
terial to us. Almost all commentators agree that the origin
of both parables is a single one told by Jesus. As Matthew
and Luke record the story with quite different elaborations, it is not difficult to determine with a fair degree of
accuracy what the original story was. A man entrusted sums
of money to three slaves, and went on a journey. When he
returned, he called the slaves to ask an accounting for
what he had given them. Two of the slaves had used the
money to good advantage, had increased the sum, and
were therefore commended. The third slave had hidden
his money and had put it to no use at all; therefore it was
taken from him and given to the slave who had the most.
The point is quite clearly that a man is to use whatever
God has given him, for God holds every man responsible.
Not to use what is given is to lose it; and to use what is
given leads to the bestowal of new gifts.

Now both Matthew and Luke have, in different ways

(and for this reason their elaborations are detectable) allegorized this parable. Jesus has become the man with the money; his return has become the Parousia; and the reckoning has become the Last Judgment. Luke inserts that the man left to receive his kingly power but was hated by his citizens and then returned with his kingly power — a reference to the incarnation and the Second Coming. Matthew adds that the third slave was cast " into the outer darkness " — an expression found only in Matthew,[21] and that there " men will weep and gnash their teeth " — an expression found once in Luke (ch. 13:28) and five other times in Matthew (chs. 8:12; 13:42, 50; 22:13; 24:51). The punishment in Matthew therefore becomes hell — the consequence of God's *Final* Judgment of guilty. Matthew has also added in two places, " Enter into the joy of your master [Lord] " by which he means heaven, another consequence of Final Judgment (Matt. 25:21, 23).

The same kind of allegorization may be seen in the parable of the ten virgins (Matt. 25:1-13), in which the bridegroom has become Christ, and his late coming has become the Parousia. A parable that originally taught preparedness has, in Matthew, been put into a radically eschatological context — just before the parable of the Last Judgment — and now teaches not preparedness, but watchfulness for the Parousia, at which time repentance will be too late (Matt. 25:11 f.).[22]

Here are two cases in which a parable or saying of Jesus has been reworked in the light of the church's expectation of the Second Coming. This kind of reorientation is a source of considerable confusion when one reads the Gospels; for, on the one hand, we have Jesus' teachings about the Kingdom of God which, one believes, are authentic; and, on the other hand, we have teachings that originally were not primarily concerned with the Kingdom but that the early church interpreted as referring directly to the Kingdom. And for the church, the Kingdom involved the Parousia. Thus were the Second Coming and Last Judgment, apocalyptically conceived, confusedly interwoven with Jesus' teaching about the Kingdom.

A further development in the early tradition was the identification of Jesus' Second Coming with the coming Son of Man whom Jews with an apocalyptic learning had expected for some time. The Book of Enoch frequently refers to a coming Elect One or Son of Man as the final judge.[23] But it was unthinkable that the church should have identified its final judge — the Messiah conceived in apocalyptic terms, the Son of Man — with anyone other than the Messiah who had come, Jesus Christ (cf. II Cor. 5:10). This identification in the Gospels of the coming Son of Man with Jesus' Second Coming is another source of confusion in trying to determine Jesus' own eschatological hopes and expectations. We must, however, separate the church's belief in the Second Coming from Jesus' belief in the coming Kingdom.

Jesus would not have taught his disciples to be prepared for the bridegroom — as he is said to have done in the parable of the ten virgins — as though he were someone who would arrive without any advance notice, totally unexpected, at an unknown time in the future. No, the Kingdom was already at hand; it had come near, and the powers of the Kingdom were already at work. Anyone who could read the signs of the times could see what was happening; it was the Father's good pleasure to give the Kingdom — now. " Ask, and it will be given you; seek, and you will find. . . . For . . . he who seeks, finds " — now! *This* is the eschatological character of Jesus' teaching. The other aspect of teaching in the Gospels, which looks for a new emergence into history quite different from anything else that has taken place, is tied up with a literalized and historicized conception of the Second Coming. And this is a part of the postresurrection faith. It cannot, I think, be attributed to Jesus.

Jesus, then, preached that God was acting decisively in the present. By " present " one does not mean simply one moment in a long chain of other similar moments. One means the *kairos,* the *time* of Jesus, the *time* of God's entrance into history in Christ, the *time* that gives meaning to chronological time. Did God act redemptively at that time? Was the time fulfilled? As a believer one answers yes, but from a point of view that could not have been shared by Jesus.

Jesus says nothing about the distant future; he speaks only about what is happening in the lives of his hearers, and about what is to happen in the immediate future. It was for later Christians, in the light of the cross, resurrection, and expected Parousia, to work out the gospel for a new community in what was to become centuries of history.

The gospel that the church was to preach could not be just a reiteration of what Jesus had preached. Jesus' emphasis was on the Kingdom that was at hand; the church's emphasis was, as we have pointed out, on what God had done, was doing, and would do in Christ. As Bultmann says, Jesus had been the bearer of his message, but after his crucifixion he became himself its essential content.[24] But it was quite clear that what had been begun had not yet been completed; that the Kingdom which had been sown a seed was not yet manifest as a tree. One early Christian put it this way: sin and evildoers are in the Kingdom with the righteous, but the " Son of man will send his angels, and they will gather [these] *out of* his kingdom " (Matt. 13:41) just as the farmer gathers weeds out of his field. Here is a conception of the Kingdom quite different from that of Jesus. It attempts to explain the presence of sin in the church and makes the unhappy identification of the church with the Kingdom, in the light of Jesus' preaching that the Kingdom was imminent. It maintains belief in the Kingdom's presence (thus assuming a literal and un-paradoxical fulfillment of Jesus' words), but it looks to the future for a purification of the Kingdom. The idea of the purification of the Kingdom followed from the iden-tification of the Kingdom with the church.

Paul, who in spite of all he said about the new creation and about the deliverance that had already taken place, nevertheless also refers either explicitly or implicitly in something like sixty-nine different places (if we include Ephesians and Colossians) to salvation under its *future* aspect. These passages reveal that Paul had not worked out any consistent, systematic conception of precisely how the salvation that had already been given was to be consum-mated. *That* there would be a consummation he fully be-lieved; but the details of how, when, and where it would take place Paul merely groped at. These were things which one could see only in a mirror, darkly. Paul was driven to say, " How inscrutable are his [God's] ways! " (Rom. 11:33) .

And not only Paul, but the pastoral epistles, Hebrews, I and II Peter, and Jude, also speak of a future fulfillment. Even the Johannine writings in which salvation is almost exclusively conceived as a present reality, and in which the judgment is understood as taking place in the present, re-fer in a few places to a future appearing and to a future

day of judgment.[25] Bultmann considers these rather isolated references to the future in the Johannine writings as
secondary; [26] but I think we must rather understand that
even John could not deny an orientation that the church
had to the future and at the same time proclaim anything
but a distorted gospel.

THE " END " AS HAVING COME AND AS YET TO COME

Now we are faced with the difficult problem, which is as
old as the church, of how to reconcile these two seemingly
contradictory points of view, found side by side throughout the whole of the New Testament. For we cannot
preach the gospel as the New Testament proclaims it and
omit either of these two emphases. We must try to understand what the New Testament as a whole has to say about
eschatology.

We have said that Jesus preached the Kingdom and the
church preached Christ. This is true if we understand
that in preaching Christ the church did not confine its
proclamation simply to a record of his life. The kerygma
included, of course, historical data about Jesus' life —
what he had said and what he had done. These accounts
were used as proof of who Jesus really was, in spite of the
fact that he had been crucified; and much of Jesus' teaching was used as a basis for the church's ethical instruction.

But in preaching Christ, the church preached more than
Jesus' historical words and deeds. It preached also the salvation that God had made and continued to make available through Christ. It is here, in connection with this
message, that the confusion between present and future
arises. Is one saved by Christ or is one not? If the believer
is saved, in what way is the future relevant to salvation?
Or, if the believer is *not* yet saved, and his salvation is de-

pendent upon what he does in the future, or upon what God is yet to do in Christ, or on a combination of the two, then in what sense is the *past* — viz., God's action in and through Jesus of Nazareth — relevant to salvation? The New Testament does not settle for either of the two alternatives implied in these questions. It consistently affirms both that God's act in the historical Jesus is decisive for salvation, and that the future remains entirely and exclusively in God's hands. The salvation given the believer in Christ must be continually reappropriated; and the life given at death is as much given by God as the life given at birth. Salvation in the New Testament is not a state of holiness; it is a relationship of reconciliation, at each new moment dependent upon man's reacceptance of the grace of God. This is why the New Testament on almost every page, and often many times on a single page, refers both to what God has done and to what God will do. Salvation depends on both.

So far, then, as the Kingdom of God is concerned, this means, as the New Testament says, that it *has* come and that it *will* come. Specific references to the "kingdom of God" are scarce outside of the Synoptic Gospels — they average less than one reference in every two books — while there are over a hundred such references in the Synoptics alone. But this is simply a matter of terminology. Whereas the Synoptics refer frequently to the Kingdom of God, other books refer to life, or salvation, or reconciliation, or glory. But all these words point in the same direction — toward the realization of the relationship that God intended men to have with him and with one another, which becomes a possibility through Christ. Where this relationship is realized, *there* is the Kingdom, salvation, reconciliation, glorification, life.

This Kingdom, then, has been given in Christ; but it is a hidden Kingdom. As the Messiah was both hidden and revealed, so the Kingdom was both hidden and revealed. The hiddenness of the Kingdom, and not only its smallness in the present world, is revealed in such passages as these: the Kingdom of God is like " leaven which a woman took and *hid* " (Luke 13:21; Matt. 13:33). Or, the Kingdom of heaven is like a treasure *hidden* in a field.[27] In this state of hiddenness, when its power is not yet revealed except to eyes that can see, the Kingdom is subject to violent attack (Matt. 11:12), just as Christ, whose Messiahship was hidden, was subject to arrest and crucifixion. But when Jesus' Messiahship was revealed to eyes that could see at the resurrection, then also the presence and power of the Kingdom were made manifest to faith. In this connection let us look at a verse that represents a view unique in Mark, except for the " Little Apocalypse ": ch. 9:1. There Jesus says, " Truly, I say to you, there are some standing here who will not taste death before they see the kingdom of God come with power."

The Kingdom of God, which during his life Jesus had preached as " at hand," had not yet " come with power " — that is, it had not yet come in such a way that men could identify it, although Jesus had himself seen it at work in his own activity, and spirits of the supernatural world had also realized that they confronted it. But because the Kingdom was hidden from the disciples (just as Jesus' Messiahship was) they could not appropriate its powers and cure the epileptic boy (Mark 9:18 and parallels). However, after the Kingdom had " come with power " at the resurrection, and the Spirit was given, then believing in its presence, as they believed for the first time with assurance in Jesus' Messiahship, they could heal.[28]

Jesus had said, " There are *some* standing here." This does not mean a few babies who might conceivably live long enough to see the Kingdom when it came with power; but it refers to those who, regardless of their years, will, when the Kingdom comes with power, have eyes to see it. Who are those " some "? They are those who were to believe that God raised Jesus from the dead. There is an inherent relation between belief in Jesus' Messiahship and belief in the presence of the Kingdom. The agent of God's rule and the rule itself become manifest at the same time. The Spirit is given at the time of the vindication of the Messiah *and* of the Messianic Kingdom. To recognize Christ as Lord is to recognize his rule and authority now, and to recognize his rule in the present is to recognize the presence of the Kingdom; for wherever and whenever God rules, there his Kingdom is. And so Paul can say that God has put all things under Christ's feet and *has made* him head over all things (Eph. 1:22) .

But it is clear that God's rule in history is at best fragmentary. There are many who neither acknowledge it nor pray for it. And even Christians, who as Paul says *are* a new creation (II Cor. 5:17 ff.) , whom God has made alive together with Christ and raised up with him, who have been made to sit with him in the heavenly places (Eph. 2:5-8) , who are being changed from one degree of glory to another (II Cor. 3:18) , even these do not yet attain (Phil. 3:12) ; they must be continually exhorted by Paul about their behavior, and are told that even they — though justified and reconciled and having peace with God (Rom. 5:1 ff.) — must yet stand before the judgment seat of God (Rom. 14:10; II Cor. 5:10) and render an account of themselves before him (Rom. 14:12) . This is so because salvation is not a possession but a gift, which in history is always being made and must be continually re-accepted. Hence Paul can speak of Christians as those "who *have been* brought from death to life" (Rom. 6:13), and yet know that the life to which they have been brought, the life which God has given them in Christ, must be given again; for if God does not raise Christians from the dead, they will not be raised (cf. I Cor. chs. 15; 6:14; II Cor. 4:14). Or, as he puts it concisely elsewhere, "God . . . delivered us . . . , and he will deliver us" (II Cor. 1:9-10).

Therefore, Christian eschatology cannot be oriented exclusively toward the future because the salvation for which the Christian hopes is already given him. The eschatological vision includes past, present, and future; it includes the beginning as well as the end. God as Redeemer cannot be abstracted in thought, permanently, from God as Creator, for redemption *is* creation and presupposes creation.

We have said that eschatology looks to the past as well as to the future because that for which the Christian hopes has already been given him in part. Paul says that the Christian has received an *arrabōn,* an earnest or guarantee of the future life (II Cor. 1:22; 5:5; Eph. 1:14). Jesus says, "Blessed are the poor in spirit, for theirs *is* the kingdom of heaven" (Matt. 5:3). Or again, Paul says that God "has qualified us to share in the inheritance of the saints in light. . . . [For] he has . . . transferred us to the kingdom of his beloved Son, in whom we have redemption" (Col. 1:12 ff.). And John hardly mentions the future because, for him, the Christian already has eternal life; and if he abides in Christ, he does not sin (I John 3:6; cf. Rom. 6:22).

But if salvation is already given, why does the Christian yet hope for it? For as Paul says: "Hope that is seen is not

hope. For who hopes for what he sees? " (Rom. 8:24.)
This is a paradox and a burden of Christian life which the
New Testament makes very plain. On the one hand, the
Christian has been raised with Christ and sits with him in
heavenly places; and on the other hand, like one who
never knew Christ, he must be admonished to abstain
from the very same sins that the rest of the world also com-
mit. Paul fears that when he visits Corinth he will find
" quarreling, jealousy, anger, selfishness, slander, gossip,
conceit, and disorder, . . . impurity, immorality, and li-
centiousness " (II Cor. 12:20 f.) — not among the pagans,
but among his converts who have received the Holy Spirit
and who, unbelievable as it may appear, are to consider
themselves " dead to sin and alive to God in Christ Jesus "
(Rom. 6:11) . The holy people of God, the saints who are
to judge the world (I Cor. 6:2) , are stained with impurity.
Christians stand in uncertain certainty with regard to the
guarantee they have received and the life that has been
given them.

But what is true of the present and the past is also true
of the future. The Christian stands proportionately as sure
of the future as he is of the past. He is as sure, and no
surer, of what God *will* do as he is of what God *has* done.
And so Paul, who can write the Romans that they have
been set free from sin (Rom. 6:22) , that God has justified
them and no other can accuse them, and that nothing in
all creation can separate them from the love of God (Rom.
8:31 ff.) , also tells them that they face a final judgment at
which they will be held responsible for all their past
(Rom. 14:10, 12) . What is certain becomes uncertain. And
so, also, the author of Hebrews writes that Christ " has appeared *once for all* at the end of the age " (Heb. 9:26) ,
and two verses later says that Christ " will appear a second

time "; and the Kingdom which is already received (Heb. 12:28) is still a promise (Heb. 9:15; 10:36; 13:14) .

The Christian stands in a position of uncertain-certainty with regard to his future as he does with regard to his present and past. Here again eschatology looks to both past and future; man is as certain of the future as he is of the past, and his hopes for the future are the same as his hopes for the past. " If Christ has not been raised, [then] your faith is futile." (I Cor. 15:17.) The Christian's faith in the future is dependent on his faith in the past. The Christian knows that Jesus is the Christ, but he knows it only by faith; and he knows that he will be raised with Christ, but he knows this, too, only by faith. He has the same degree of certainty in the one that he has in the other — a certainty that, because the world will never affirm it but will always seek to undermine it, must ever remain a hope.

We have said that the New Testament affirms that the Kingdom has come, that believers are raised with Christ, and that salvation is given to those who have faith, but that the New Testament also looks forward to the coming of the Kingdom, to a future resurrection with Christ, and to a future salvation that remains dependent on the grace of God. This is because salvation is not a state but a relationship, and the life of the believer bears witness to the fact that the salvation into which he has entered must needs be fulfilled. The New Testament, from Jesus to the final Apocalypse, looks forward to a consummation of what has been begun in Christ.

Moreover, the character of the end is revealed to Christians as it is revealed to no others. For example, that to which the Old Testament and later Jewish writings look forward is a state or condition that is quite different from

anything known in the Jewish past. The idealized picture
of the exodus and of the Hebrews' entrance into Canaan,
drawn by the priestly writers and by the Deuteronomic editors of the J–E narratives, does not correspond to the data
recorded much earlier by the Yahwist. But in the New
Testament, history fulfills the pattern that Christ, known
in history, has imposed upon it. The character of the Kingdom, what the Kingdom is like, is already revealed and
is to be seen, for the Christians, in Christ. The values of
the Kingdom are Christ's values; life in the Kingdom is
life as Christ lived it. In Christ, men see what God's claim
upon them is in the Kingdom, and what it means to be
obedient.

For the Christian, the end refers to the revealing of the
absolute rule of Christ. The end will involve neither the
rule of a new Lord not yet known — some expected but
still unknown Messiah or Son of Man — nor a new and
different rule to be set up by the Lord already known. No,
the end for the Christian points rather to the full and complete manifestation of him whose rule is already known by
faith.

We shall be aided, I think, in understanding the Christian conception of the end if we contrast it with other
views:

1. There is the cyclical view of history which was characteristic of the Greeks and which followed perhaps inevitably from their cosmology. According to this view,
history has no end, but represents a world cycle that will
one day begin all over again. In his historical existence,
man is simply repeating in the present world cycle what he
has done before in another world cycle, and will do still
again. The cycles themselves have no meaning; they do
not progress, nor do they ever culminate in anything. And

so, according to this view, historical existence can have no ultimate meaning.

2. Linear views of history are more popular today, and theologians often embrace them as characteristic of the Old and New Testaments. But I think that in neither is the understanding of history, strictly speaking, linear. According to the New Testament, the " end " of the linear line has already appeared at the center of the line. It is not yet fully revealed, but it has nonetheless appeared; and when the end shall be fully seen, then shall the center also be disclosed.

A criticism that I should make of linear views of history is that according to such views, once the end is inaugurated, the historical process that culminates in the end tends to lose its meaning, or at least any *ultimate* meaning. History cannot have more than a relative significance. Ultimate significance is attributed only to the end. But in the New Testament, since the end has entered the middle of the line, the line itself can no longer be sloughed off at its end. The line cannot be a means to an end when the end is also at the center of the line. History does not give place, then, to the new age, but is taken into that age, for all things are united in Christ (Eph. 1:10). All historical events have ultimate meaning as they are related, not just to the end in which they issue, but also to the middle and to the beginning; for the center of history, which will be revealed at the end, was also " in the beginning " as well (John 1:2). Salvation, therefore, cannot be ultimately separated from creation; Alpha and Omega are one; Jesus Christ is the same yesterday, today, and forever (Rev. 21:6; 22:13; Heb. 13:8).

History cannot on the Christian view be said to *issue* in the Kingdom of God; nor can the Kingdom be thought of as the final historical period. The relationship between the Kingdom and history cannot be merely one of succession; for the Kingdom, which is to come, has already come proleptically; and the Messiah who will rule in that Kingdom, already rules proleptically. The believer does not leave this world to receive the Kingdom. He can receive it here because God meets him here in Christ. Jesus Christ is his assurance that God has entered history and that life is being redeemed. And the figure of the Lamb in heaven, standing as though it had been slain (Rev. 5:6) symbolizes God's receiving the events of history in heaven where their ultimate meaning is disclosed. In the Apocalypse, heaven and earth, time and eternity, are so intimately related that time seems on occasion to lose its meaning. The Lamb is slain before the tragedies of history ever begin, and the whole of history is viewed at a glance. But time does not lose its meaning, it receives it in its relation to eternity.

The Kingdom of God broke into history in Christ in a final and absolute way. The church is not given the authority to proclaim that in some future historical period the Kingdom will be manifest on earth in a form superior to its manifestation in Christ. If this could be, then the revelation in Christ was not final, but only a precursor to the final revelation in history. The Kingdom is as closely related to the present as it will be to any period of history. We do not believe that the event of Christ can be harmonized with a linear view of history that looks to a future historical period for final revelation. Furthermore, historical existence and the Kingdom of God can never be identical. Essential to historical existence are separation or estrangement and uncertainty, and universal acknowledgment of Christ in any historical period cannot remove these conditions.

The prayer that God's Kingdom will come " on earth as it is in heaven " is a prayer that Jesus taught his disciples to pray as long as they remain within history. It is not a prayer to abolish historical life, and the conditions under which it must be lived, and to institute the Kingdom of God in its place, but is a prayer — which, incidentally, always remains a prayer and never becomes a commentary — that God's will may be done on earth, in history, as it is in heaven. The Christian community is taught to pray that it may act within history, under the conditions of historical life, in accordance with the revealed will of God; and wherever its activity corresponds to this will, there God's will prevails, he rules, and his Kingdom is revealed. This is not a prayer that the Christian's freedom of action will be taken from him, that God will overrule the believer's will and so arbitrarily set up his Kingdom. It is a prayer that God will rule *in* history; that is, that I and the community of saints will choose to do God's will. Nor is this prayer concerned primarily with the far-distant future — that centuries or millenniums hence God's Kingdom will come. It is a prayer immediately relevant to me and to my time, to the church of today, that God will rule, now, in me as a believer and in the church as the body of Christ, on earth as he does in heaven.

This interpretation of Jesus' prayer, as a prayer for the present and not for the millennium, does not stymie action or lead to pessimism; for if one understands aright the meaning of the Christ-event, of God's entrance into history in Christ, one will not underestimate and one cannot overestimate the significance of every decision and of every commitment.

But the Christian cannot forget, either in this age or in any age, that the peace that Christ bestows, which passes understanding, will always pass the understanding of natural man. It is only in faith that this peace can be appropriated, and even the saints often pass it by. To be a Christian is now, as it has always been, to take up the cross of Christ. And to everyone who takes it up Christ says, now, as he did to his first disciples: " The cup that I drink you will drink; and with the baptism with which I am baptized, you will be baptized " (Mark 10:39). " I send you out as sheep in the midst of wolves " (Matt. 10:16) ; and " Lo I am with you always " (Matt. 28:20).

The end of the historical process could well be similar to the end of the historical life of Jesus. It may be characterized by a like sorrow and suffering. But this would not mean either that the whole development had been meaningless, or that from the divine perspective it would not be consummated. From the point of view of man it might appear tragic, but from God's point of view it must be victorious.

The events that the New Testament expects to occur in the last days affirm not only God's final Lordship over history but his present and past Lordship and creativity as well. They point to the faith that what has meaning in history from the point of view of Christ has ultimate meaning from the point of view of God. New Testament eschatology affirms that all such meanings are validated in heaven; that *agapē* cannot ultimately fail or be defeated; and that life worked out in fear and trembling, with God also at work, is eternal.

X

Jesus' Pre-existence and Virgin Birth

THE EXISTENTIAL CRITERION

The New Testament kerygma is proclaimed in the language of myth, and we believe that the essential truth of the kerygma cannot be communicated in any other language. We also believe, however, that the myths must be interpreted, but always in harmony with their original intention and context. Moreover, we agree with Bultmann to the extent that the kerygma must be interpreted in terms of the life and faith of believers. But in many cases this relation is indirect. There are myths in the New Testament whose purpose is to speak primarily about God, Christ, or the world, and only secondarily about man. The fact that they speak about God, Christ, or the world does not, however, mean that they describe an objective truth that has no existential meaning for men; but the existential meaning is derived as a secondary one from the truth which it was the myth's primary intention to convey.

Bultmann interprets only those myths whose primary meaning is existential, for it is only those which he can demythologize. We suggest, however, that nonanthropological myths have a derived existential significance that enlarges our understanding of the meaning of the kerygma. Myths should not be eliminated because their central meaning does not concern man, or because their primary significance is not an existential one. Barth is right in saying that theological statements deal with more than the Christian understanding of man.[1] But theological statements are meaningless if they cannot be related to the life of man. Bultmann is right in understanding this, but he has failed to see the relevance for man — the existential meanings — to be derived from theological and cosmological, as well as anthropological, myths; and he has also frequently limited the meanings of the myths that he has interpreted to a single, existential one. We suggest that no New Testament myths should be eliminated, for they all augment the meaning and significance of the kerygma. We also suggest that events be interpreted in accordance with the several meanings that the New Testament often ascribes to them, and not in terms of only one of these meanings, as Bultmann is wont to do.

Let us now consider the mythological language in which Jesus' pre-existence and birth are represented in the New Testament. Bultmann considers Jesus Christ " as the Son of God, as a pre-existent divine being " to be a " mythical figure," [2] just as he also considers the stories of the virgin birth to be mythological.[3] But since Bultmann sees no existential meaning in these myths, he eliminates them as a meaningless part of the kerygma. We propose, however, that the elimination of these myths weakens the total message of the kerygma and decreases its authentic meaning.

The Virgin Birth

The stories of the virgin birth found in Matthew and Luke may be described as legends, for they are unhistorical elaborations, within the tradition, of the historical event of Jesus' birth. But they are also mythological in character, for they are dramatic representations of the activity of God in history. They point to the belief that God was related uniquely to this particular birth as to no other, and that this child was related uniquely to the God and Father of mankind. The truth of the story of the virgin birth does not stand or fall on the ability of science to prove or disprove its occurrence, for the story is not a historical, scientific statement accounting for a unique biological event in the ancient world. It is, rather, a mythological statement of faith asserting the entrance of the divine into human history in Jesus Christ, and science knows nothing of the truth or falsity of such an event.

The belief in the divinity of Christ was not derived from the story of the virgin birth,[4] but the story of the virgin birth was derived from a belief in the divinity of Christ. The story ought not be used as a proving miracle, for it has no meaning apart from faith, and cannot prove the truth of faith. It originally grew out of faith, and is therefore believable only in faith. The story ought not, then, be interpreted literally. Such an interpretation would remove it from the realm of faith into the realm of history. But neither should the story be eliminated as meaningless to modern man. It is not meaningless precisely because it is not scientific. It is mythological, and as a myth it augments the content of Christian faith by speaking about the divine aspect of the birth of Him who was born for the redemption of the world.

To pretend to discuss in a few pages the birth narratives of Matthew and Luke in any detail would be outrageously presumptuous, for literature on this subject is enormous — discouragingly so.[5] But perhaps a few words on the birth stories in connection with our theme would not be altogether out of place; and it is hoped that brevity will be excused.

We may begin by noting that the virgin birth of Jesus is nowhere referred to in the New Testament except in the birth narratives of Matthew and Luke, and that neither Matthew nor Luke even alludes to a virgin birth except in these narratives. Furthermore, of the two gospels, Matthew stresses the virgin birth more than Luke. In Luke, for example, immediately after the birth of Jesus is recounted, Joseph is called Jesus' father (Luke 2:33), and Mary and Joseph are three times called Jesus' "parents" (Luke 2:27, 41, 43). It is very clear that Luke was not interested in pressing, systematically, Jesus' birth of a virgin, which had for him a mythological rather than a logical meaning.

The stories of Jesus' birth in Matthew are, of course, quite different from the Nativity stories in Luke. They originated in different areas of the church and have no inherent, inner unity either with each other or with any other material in their respective Gospels. In connection with the latter point, it is notable that the virgin birth stories quite contradict and, if taken literally, render pointless the genealogies of both Matthew and Luke. In both Gospels Jesus' genealogy is traced back through Joseph. The virgin birth stories have no inherent relation to the genealogical lists.

In Luke, Jesus' genealogy is not given in connection with the birth stories at all, but is inserted much later — after a story of Jesus' childhood, and Luke's account of John's message and of Jesus' baptism. Furthermore, there is nothing in Luke's genealogy that would lead one to believe that Jesus was born of a virgin except the words "as was supposed" (Luke 3:23), which one is forced to conclude were inserted in the genealogy after the latter was attached to the virgin birth story. It would have been somewhat pointless to trace Jesus' genealogy back through Joseph if it had been known when the genealogy was composed that the " supposition " that Joseph was Jesus' father was in error. No; the genealogy found in Luke did not originally assume that Jesus was born of a virgin. In fact, it assumed that Joseph was Jesus' father.

If we turn to Jesus' genealogy as recorded in Matthew, we find that here the genealogy is juxtaposed to the birth narrative (immediately preceding it) but, again, that it does not assume Jesus was born of a virgin. Once again, the genealogy is traced back through Joseph; but later copyists and " editors " altered Matt. 1:16 to make it read that Jesus was born of a virgin. Fortunately, however, we have an unimproved reading.

Returning to the birth stories proper, it has been noted that Luke does not emphasize Jesus' birth of a *virgin* to the extent that Matthew does. We must not be misled in this regard by the two appearances in Luke 1:27 of the word " virgin " (the only verse in which the word occurs in Luke). The narrative here simply indicates (unless one assumes the later Christian dogma of the perpetual virginity of Mary) that Gabriel appeared to Mary before she had had sexual relations with Joseph to whom she was then betrothed. But since Mary was betrothed at the time of Gabriel's appearance, the assumption would be that in only a matter of months she would have relations with Joseph, for betrothals of virgins were not to exceed twelve months.[6] So Gabriel's appearance to a " virgin " does not in itself preclude the possibility of Joseph's being Jesus' father. And Luke 1:31 — " You will conceive in your womb and bear a son " — may simply be a prophecy of a child that Mary is to have by Joseph, to whom she is betrothed.

It is only Luke 1:35 which, when read in connection with ch. 1:34, implies a virgin birth. But v. 34 creates a logical difficulty in the story. Mary's question, " How can this be, since I have no husband? " is utterly naïve. Gabriel has not said that Mary would conceive at that moment, but only that she would conceive in the future; and Mary's conception in the near future is altogether possible, as she must know, because she is betrothed. But it is only in the light of this somewhat illogical question in v. 34 that Gabriel's answer in v. 35 may be read as indicating the imminence of a virgin birth. Otherwise the whole narrative reminds one of Sarah's conception of Isaac in Gen., ch. 18 ff. In Sarah's case the expectation of conception has been given up because she and Abraham are too old; in Mary's case there is no expectation of conception because she is still only betrothed. But in both cases the power of God makes conception possible. In Genesis the Lord asks Abraham whether anything is impossible with God (Gen. 18:14) ; and in Luke it is Gabriel who tells Mary, quoting the LXX of Genesis, that nothing is impossible with God (Luke 1:37) . In both Genesis and Luke there is an annunciation, and the angel's words to Mary, " You have found favor with God " (Luke 1:30) are a clear reminiscence of the LXX of Genesis where Abraham asks whether he has " found favor " with the Lord (Gen. 18:3) . Once again, a question in the Genesis narrative becomes a statement in Luke. Gabriel's next statement to Mary, " Behold, you will conceive in your womb and bear a son, and you shall call his name Jesus " (Luke 1:31) is, except for the change in the proper name, and except for the verb " you will conceive," an exact quotation from the LXX of Gen. 16:11 — the angel's words to Hagar (cf. also Isa. 7:14) .

Luke's narrative reveals a good deal of reflection on the subject of Jesus' birth, with the LXX, as well as writings in Hebrew, close at hand. Luke does not *stress* the virgin-ity of Mary, although in its present form his birth narra-tive must be said to assume it. But Luke does not press the logical implications of Jesus' birth of a virgin, not even in the second chapter immediately after he has recorded the event of Jesus' birth. Luke is interested primarily in paint-ing a picture of the new, creative act of God, the coming of the Holy Spirit, by which power the Holy One, the Son of God, came into the world. The concept of the Spirit's coming and acting is thoroughly Hebraic. The new thing is that it has come in the eschatological age. Mary's con-ception of the Messiah is the work of the Holy Spirit.

We shall not look at Matthew's birth narrative in detail. In his Gospel, Jesus' birth is depicted primarily in terms of the fulfillment of the prophecy of Isa. 7:14. Matthew's record of Jesus' birth is quite different from Luke's; but in Matthew, as in Luke, the birth is interpreted in terms of the creative act of the Holy Spirit (Matt. 1:18, 20). Also in Matthew as in Luke, no logical implications of the vir-gin birth are drawn. Matthew, like Luke, is satisfied to describe Jesus' birth in mythological terms and to leave it at that, quite naïvely. The Christian of a more enlightened age knows that the picture drawn points beyond itself, that the meanings of the words used must not be narrowly circumscribed, and that in fact it is a truth that the Holy Child was a gift of God.

THE PRE-EXISTENCE

References to Christ's pre-existence found in Paul's let-ters, Hebrews, and the Gospel of John are, like the virgin birth narratives, mythological. They speak not of Jesus' appearance on the earth, but of his eternal existence with God. They say that he through whom the world is re-deemed is also he through whom it was created. The church knew that only God, and not a created being, could redeem, and it is not the nature of divinity to be created. But if redemption is made possible through Christ, then Christ cannot be a created being having his origin in some historical period, but he must in some way be God. The Logos which became flesh in Christ " was God " (John 1:1). It was several centuries before this faith was explicitly elaborated; but it was intuited and known implicitly before a generation had passed after Christ's death. He who will be related to the last things must also have been related to the first things; the Redeemer must be the Creator; Alpha and Omega are one.

The story of Jesus' pre-existence points to the eternal divinity of the Savior.[7] The virgin birth story tells of the entrance into this world of the redeeming Christ, and is a symbol of the metahistorical fact of the divine Sonship. The two stories are not of one piece; they have different origins and different intentions. They are independent statements of faith. They both began and were first told within the community of faith, and were, for those who already believed, elaborations of the implications and meaning of the central kerygma. They should never be used as proof of the truth of the kerygma, for this was not their original purpose, as it is certainly not their function. These stories are meaningful only for those who already believe, and they should not be eliminated. Their meaning is that he through whom salvation is offered is he who alone can save — Jesus Christ, the Son of God (Mark 1:1; Heb. 1:2), only begotten of the Father (John 1:14), in whom all the fullness of God was pleased to dwell (Col. 1:19), through whom all things were created (Col. 1:16; Heb. 1:2), who was with God in the beginning, who was God (John 1:1).

XI

The Crucifixion

FREEDOM AND THE CROSS

Bultmann interprets the meaning of the crucifixion as " the freeing judgment over men " which " has created a new historical situation; the preaching of the cross as the event of salvation asks the hearer whether . . . he will be crucified with Christ." [1] Bultmann selects this Pauline interpretation of the crucifixion, which makes salvation possible for those who will die with Christ and be raised to a new life (a new " self-understanding "), as its only meaning; for this is the existential meaning of the cross. This is the meaning that remains after demythologization. In Chapter IV, we discussed this interpretation and some of the major criticisms that have been brought against it. We agreed with Bultmann that the cross is confronted in the preached Word; and we agree also that one of the New Testament's principal interpretations of the meaning of the crucifixion is the Pauline understanding of it as revealing the way of salvation in terms of dying with Christ — dying to oneself and to the world — and of being raised with him to a new life of freedom and of self-fulfillment. In dying with Christ a man reorients his life away from the transitory and the perishing things of this world with which he must also perish so long as he clings to them. He thus becomes " otherworldly," not by becoming aloof from the world and by failing to be involved in the affairs of the world, but by refusing ultimate loyalty to the things of the world which are passing away.

The existentialist Gabriel Marcel has differentiated these two types of detachment from the world — one as characteristic of the spectator, the other as describing the saint. In the case of the spectator, the knower removes himself at a distance from the objects of his investigations, maintaining control over them without involving himself personally in them. This spectator attitude is necessary in science but inadequate when applied to metaphysics and morals. In the case of the saint, however, detachment means closer participation, the saint withdrawing from the world " only in the sense of denying it his primary loyalty: he attaches himself (rather) to the creative source of the world and thus allies himself with the world from the divine perspective." [2] In dying with Christ, he not only dies to the world but also dies to himself — that is, he lives not out of his own power, but by the creative and sustaining power of God, knowing that he did not create and cannot perpetuate his life.

For man to attempt to live out of his own power, believing that his life is in his own hands to be fulfilled and sustained, or to be wasted away in final death — this is the root of all sin. It is making himself God, and looking to himself for the life that he cannot give; hence it must lead to death. But when a man dies with Christ, he orients his life toward and lives out of the Source of all life, and therefore knows that he cannot perish with the perishable but that whether he lives or whether he dies he is with Christ. He is free from the transitory — the world and himself — and oriented toward a future that is always open. The more he denies ultimate loyalty to the world and lives out of the grace of God, the freer he becomes and the more fully he may live. And, conversely, the more one lives out of the things of the world, the nearer one approaches to slavery and death.[3] For those who believe, therefore, Christ's death is a ransom (Mark 10:45) by which man is freed from " principalities " and " powers," from " things present " and " things to come " (Rom. 8:38) . It is the crucifixion and resurrection of Christ that reveals, to those who believe, this understanding of the way in which one may fully live and which makes possible participation in eternal life.

But the New Testament says more about the meaning of the crucifixion than this. It speaks also about the judgment and justice of God, and about the love of God — all of which were revealed uniquely in history in the death of Christ. Bultmann understands the crucifixion as revealing the judgment of God, for in revealing the possibility of life it judges man's former understanding of his life and shows him the way in which, alone, he may truly live.[4] But Bultmann says nothing about the revelation of the love of God, or about the cross as having been in any sense a sacrifice. He writes, " The idea of an atonement and the teaching of a satisfaction are juridical; and the application of such concepts to God is mythology." [5] As Bultmann is unable to demythologize these concepts, they can find no place in his understanding of the meaning of the crucifixion. But it is our belief that the significance of these concepts is not to be given up simply because the mythological language in which they are expressed seems unavoidable.

SACRIFICE AND THE CROSS

Let us consider the crucifixion as in some way atoning for sin. Bultmann will not grant that the idea of atonement can have existential meaning to modern man, and the idea of sacrifice is increasingly difficult for believers to appropriate as a relevant part of the gospel. The question is whether or not Jesus' crucifixion, understood as a sacrifice, is a central aspect of the New Testament kerygma and can be made understandable to contemporary man.

Before we deal with these questions we must inquire more specifically into what the New Testament does not say about the cross as atoning for sin. We do not want to defend as kerygma what was not preached as such. It is important to note that the New Testament does not understand the crucifixion as propitiating — that is, as appeasing — an angry God. We should make a distinction between " propitiation " and " expiation." To propitiate is " to appease or conciliate, to render favorable " (cf. the adjective " propitious ") ; to expiate is " to make satisfaction for or atone for sin." The word is also used to represent the idea conveyed by the Hebrew *kipper*, " to cover." The New Testament refers to the expiation of sin made on Calvary; it does not refer to the propitiation of an avenging God.

But the understanding of the crucifixion as in some way a sacrifice for sin is, so far as can be discerned, the church's oldest understanding of the reason for Calvary and of what happened there between God and man. It may have been that in the earliest days of the church, when some of Jesus' original disciples first came profoundly to believe that their crucified Master was the long-expected Messiah, that the significance of the resurrection was believed in before any meaning at all was attributed to the crucifixion. In his speech recorded in Acts 2:22-36, Peter mentions the crucifixion only as a historical event, and ascribes no meaning or significance to it other than that it

occurred "according to the definite plan and foreknowledge of God."[6] He attributes a soteriological meaning
only to the resurrection — namely, that in the resurrection it is shown that God has made Jesus "both Lord and
Christ" (Acts 2:36).

But very early, just when we do not know, the crucifixion was understood as a sacrifice for sin, in continuity with
the Jewish sacrificial system. Such an interpretation of Calvary was undoubtedly in the pre-Pauline tradition, which
was handed down to the apostle and which he, himself,
adopted as a part of his interpretation of the cross. Paul
wrote to the Corinthians, "I delivered to you as of first
importance what I also received, that Christ died for our
sins in accordance with the scriptures" (I Cor. 15:3).
Here Paul referred to the tradition that he had received
(a pre-Pauline tradition), which had related Jesus' death
to the sin of man. Also, to the Romans, Paul wrote that
all men are justified by the grace of God as a gift, "through
the redemption which is in Christ Jesus, whom God put
forward as an expiation by his blood, to be received by
faith (Rom. 3:24 ff.). For Paul, sacrifice was necessarily involved in reconciliation, and God's judgment on sin was
not compromised in his forgiveness.[7]

In the letter to the Hebrews the understanding of the
crucifixion as a sacrifice is greatly stressed; in fact it may
be said to be "the most fundamental note in the teaching
of the epistle."[8] The author writes that Christ "entered
once for all into the Holy Place, taking not the blood of
goats and calves but his own blood, thus securing an eternal redemption" (Heb. 9:12). And again, "The blood of
Christ, who . . . offered himself without blemish to God,
[will] purify your conscience from dead works to serve the
living God" (Heb. 9:14); that is, the blood of Christ re-

moves the burden of guilt from the shoulders of those who believe, and sets them free without the unbearable weight of the consciousness of sin for which they can never atone — free to serve the living God. This is an understanding of the atonement in terms of the Jewish sacrificial system according to which a sacrifice to God, in this case Jesus' self-sacrifice, atones for sin, assures forgiveness, and relieves from the burden of guilt, with the knowledge that God's just requirement has been fulfilled. Why God should have made such a requirement was a question that was not asked in tannaitic Judaism; nor was a theory worked out as to the way in which sacrifices atoned for sin. God simply revealed certain conditions on which he would remit sins; and for one to refuse to meet these conditions because he knew not how they could be effective was to sin the more.[9]

The church, then, at the very beginning, began to interpret Jesus' crucifixion in terms of sacrifice. The roots of this interpretation lay deep in Judaism. We must therefore inquire into the meaning of sacrifice in Judaism if we are to begin to understand why the early church adopted this concept, and what the church meant by it. We cannot discard prematurely such a basic New Testament understanding of the cross, and we have acted prematurely if we have not first attempted to become acquainted with the soil from which the concept was taken and developed.

The *origin* of the temple cult in Judaism is not of primary importance for our purposes; for whatever its origin, and however inspired or misguided its early development may be said to have been, it was of the first importance in the piety of the Jews long before the Christian era. Already in Ezekiel the cult is interpreted as having been instituted by God, and as making demands of man that he is required to fulfill (cf. Ezek. 20:40 f.) .

The sacrifices were the most important aspect of the
temple cult, for it was in the sacrifices that the process of
the purification of the Israelite reached its culmination.
We must then note some of the symbolism involved in
Jewish sacrifices. We should stress, in the first place, that
in the ancient world the " sacrifice " was a religious concept that did not connote primarily deprivation, reluc-
tance, renunciation, or sadness, but instead connoted joy,
festivity, communion, and thanksgiving. The stress was on
the *giving,* and not on the giving *up*. And, most important,
the death incurred in the case of animal sacrifice was not
usually thought of as a factor (or, at least, as an important
factor) in the sacrifice itself. It was rather considered to be
a necessary preliminary to the sacrifice.[10] If we think of a
contemporary meal at which meat is eaten, the slaughtering of the animal is not an aspect of the meal itself; it is
simply an assumed preliminary to the meal (if, indeed, it
is thought of at all) . The animal, of course, cannot be
eaten if it has not first been killed. So it was, for the most
part, with ancient sacrifices. The slaughtering of the animal and the animal's death were not usually considered a
major aspect (or any aspect at all) of the sacrifice. This
was true also in Judaism where two elements of primary
importance were the offering of the blood and the communal eating of the meat. I want now to speak only of the
former — the offering of the blood.[11]

When the animal was slaughtered, the blood was sprinkled on the altar or holy stone. God's presence was believed to be uniquely related to these. The blood, we must
remember, was not to be eaten by Jews (cf. Deut. 15:23) ;
it represented the victim's life: " The life of the flesh is in
the blood " (Lev. 17:11) . What was offered in sacrifice,

then, was not a dead animal but the *life* of the animal; and
this was offered to God in a direct way when the blood
made contact with the altar. In this way the offspring of the
animal were sanctified,[12] but the one who made the offering also shared in the sanctification. It was believed that
the offering of life to the Creator of life led, in a cyclical
way, to the Creator's restoring of life. Nothing less than
life for life would do; and the offering of human life,
which is more than once referred to in the Old Testament,
was motivated from the same premises.[13]

But to return to the matter of the reception of life by
means of the life offered in sacrifice: the one who made the
sacrifice laid his hand upon the head of the victim. " By
this act he establishes the fact that the animal is his prop-
erty. It belongs to his sphere, and when it is sanctified, the
sanctification primarily affects him. . . . The actual sanctification, on the other hand, was performed by the priests.
They received the blood and sprinkled it round the altar." [14] The laying of the hands on the head of the victim
was one of the few acts performed in the ritual — in burnt
offerings (Lev. 1:4), peace offerings (Lev. 3:2), and sin
offerings (Lev. 4:4). The effect of the offering was both
positive and negative: it "strengthened the blessing
through sanctification, but the negative side, corresponding to this, i.e., purging the soul of evil, of sin and the
curse, is the essential element in the action of the sin-
offering." [15]

The point we wish to emphasize, because of its immediate relevance to one of the most significant New Testament interpretations of the crucifixion, is the Jewish assumption that life must be offered to God in order to be
received from him, and the Jewish symbolic identification
of the life of the one who makes the sacrifice with the life

of the victim which is sacrificed.

In the New Testament the crucifixion commonly represents a ransom, or an offering made, or a price paid. The idea of blood having been poured out in order that life be made whole is too deeply embedded in New Testament thought to be dismissed without a careful analysis first being made of what was intended by such a concept. Paul, for example (to cite one author), writes that Christians have been " bought with a price " (I Cor. 6:20; 7:23), that they are made righteous by Christ's blood (Rom. 5:9), that Christ died " for our sins " (I Cor. 15:3; II Cor. 5:14), or " for us " (Rom. 5:6, 8; 14:15; I Thess. 5:10; cf. I Cor. 1:13), that Jesus was " given up " or " gave himself up " for us (Rom. 4:25; 8:32; Gal. 1:4; 2:20).

Let us now look more particularly at Rom. 3:24 ff. Here Paul writes that we are made righteous as a gift, by the grace of God, through the *ransoming* that is in Christ Jesus. In the Old Testament when God is said to ransom or redeem, he is not said to offer a price. He ransoms by grace, but gives nothing as an equivalent. The exception to this is in Isa. 43:3 ff. where we are told that God gave Egypt as a ransom, Ethiopia and Seba in exchange for Israel: " I give men in return for you, peoples in exchange for your life." So, also, according to Paul, God offered Jesus as a ransom, as the price by which he not only woos back, but — more important still — re-creates the life of the people of God; for in his ransom God put forward Christ Jesus as " an expiation by his blood," or, perhaps better, as " a blood-expiation." This is not simply the offering of forgiveness. It *is* that, but it is also more than that. Here is a blood-offering for sin, the blood of the victim poured out on the altar called Golgotha, by which *life* (for the blood is the *life*) man may receive life. The believer

associates his life with the life of the victim, not by touching the victim's head, but " by faith," by identifying his
life, in faith, with the life poured out, by " dying with
Christ."

We must also note that in the new covenant it is *God*
who offers or " puts forward " the victim (Rom. 3:25;
cf. Rom. 5:8; 8:31 f., 39; II Cor. 5:14) ; it is not man. In
the Jewish cult it was the sinner who brought before God
the life that was to be poured out on the altar; but, says
Paul, at the crucifixion *God* offered the blood, the life that
saves all who will receive it by faith. Life which God himself offered was poured out for the re-creation of life.

RECONCILIATION AND THE CROSS

The cross is such a commonplace to us in the church
that we are almost totally numbed to the horror of it. We
have mentioned a view, which persisted for centuries in
Israel, that God demanded the sacrifice of first-born sons.
But the practice was apparently never widespread, though
there seems to have been a revival of child sacrifices
around 600 B.C. (cf. Jer. 7:31; 19:5; 32:35; Ezek. 16:20;
23:37 ff.) . Jeremiah and Ezekiel, however, both strongly
condemned the practice, and there is no reason to believe
that it persisted for long. At any rate, by the time of the
Christian era human sacrifice had long been considered an
appalling barbarism. Paul had to interpret — to himself,
first, and then to others — how it came about that the
Messiah was *crucified!* He had not only suffered, he had
been nailed to a criminal's cross! Who had done this? Who
permitted it? Had strong and ruthless men determined the
fate of Jesus while God wrung his hands far away? Is the
crucifixion a sign that all things good and pure and beautiful must either spoil or lose their glory, or else be

crushed by the world's barbarity? Most certainly not! Paul
said quite the reverse: God himself made the offering, the
human sacrifice, the sacrifice of none other than the Messiah. And Paul also said, without contradicting himself,
that Christ offered *himself*. It was, in fact, precisely in this
offering — God of Christ and Christ of himself — this offering on behalf of *enemies,* that Paul saw the crucifixion
as the supreme revelation of the love of God. There is
horror here; but if one looks long enough, one may begin
to understand the mystery that there is no forgiveness
without the shedding of blood (Heb. 9:22). *Who* must
shed the blood if man is to be reconciled to God? Who is
willing to shed it?

There is another element in the understanding of the
crucifixion as God's offering of Christ which we must note
in conclusion. It appears in Rom. 3:25b f. where Paul continues by stating that the blood-offering was made in order
to show God's righteousness, for, in his forbearance, God
had neglected former sins. *Now,* however, God reveals that
his " passing over " of sins does not indicate his indiffer-
ence to sin. On the contrary, God is " righteous," which
in this context is the equivalent of saying that he is a God
of wrath as well as of love. Both his wrath and his love are
revealed in the crucifixion, and, in fact, they are not different " aspects " or " characteristics " of God. It is the
same act that both reconciled and made " to be sin one
who knew no sin " (cf. II Cor. 5:21). In saying, then, that
the expiation in the blood of Christ was to show God's
righteousness, Paul is saying that God's acquittal of the
sinner is not to be construed as revealing a tolerant indif-
ference to the distinction between obedience and disobedi-
ence which God makes, as God. Love for God and rebel-
lion against him remain opposites, and God in Christ does

not equate them. The seriousness of sin is in no way di-
minished by the revelation on Calvary; on the contrary,
it is heightened to a dimension never before revealed so
clearly. If sin is of little significance, then the lengths to
which God would have gone to redeem men would not
have been great; but God spared not his own Son. The understanding of the cross as a sacrifice reveals the seriousness of sin in God's sight, the resultant consequences of it,
and the overwhelming grace of God, which has so dealt
with sin as to create the possibility of setting man free. It
reveals that he who takes seriously the difference between
love and hate can believe that the judgment of guilty will
not be passed on him because it has already been passed
on Christ (II Cor. 5:21).

But to understand the crucifixion as in some way a sacrifice for sin is possible only within the community of
faith. It is quite meaningless outside of this community.
James Denney wrote:

> If I were sitting on the end of the pier, on a summer day,
> enjoying the sunshine and the air, and someone came
> along and jumped into the water and got drowned " to
> prove his love for me," I should find it quite unintelli-
> gible. I might be much in need of love, but an act in no
> rational relation to any of my necessities could not
> prove it.[16]

Only the believing Christian can understand what the expression " Christ died for thee " means. A man cannot see
the point unless he is led by God into the redemptive fel-
lowship in whose context alone meaning is illuminated.

The crucifixion, however, reveals not only the seriousness of sin; it also reveals the character of the love of God
which deals with sin. Paul wrote to the Romans that " God
shows his love for us in that while we were yet sinners

Christ died for us " (Rom. 5:8) . This statement, of course, assumes the mythological story of the pre-existence of the Son of God who, having become man and having lived a sinless life, was obedient to his Father even unto death. But the cross is the revelation of the love of God, not simply because of a literally interpreted mythological pre-supposition of Christ's Sonship, but because if it is reve-lation at all (as Bultmann agrees it is) , it is revelation of suffering. The cross says that reconciliation between God and man was not possible save through suffering. No one can read the Gospels through without repeatedly being made aware of the suffering entailed in God's great re-demptive act in Jesus Christ who " learned obedience through what he suffered " (Heb. 5:8) ; and this suffering reached its climax on Calvary —

> Did e'er such love and sorrow meet,
> Or thorns compose so rich a crown? [17]

If God revealed himself on Calvary — if this was more than just another crucifixion in the eastern Roman Em-pire — then he must have been involved in the suffering there. But the only motive that leads to voluntary suffer-ing on behalf of others is love.

Furthermore, by revealing the seriousness of sin, the cross also points to the significance of God's forgiveness; for the need of forgiveness that is felt is always proportion-ate to the estimation of the sin. Only a man who takes sin seriously can know what it means to be forgiven, can be-gin to understand what it means to say that God forgives. For forgiveness presupposes both suffering and love. To forgive, to bear away sin, involves voluntary submission to the burden of sin; and this is done only in love, for it en-tails the willingness to accept suffering. It is only when forgiveness is so understood that a man begins to perceive how extraordinary it is that God should forgive. It is the Lord God Almighty who becomes a slave, and carries off man's sin. Here, then, in another way, the love of God is revealed on the cross; salvation is granted to those who are forgiven, but only love forgives.

One sees that it is not possible to demythologize even the crucifixion; for even on Bultmann's single interpretation of its significance, mythological elements are presupposed. Bultmann writes, " To believe in the cross means to assume the cross of Christ as one's own, that is, to be crucified with Christ." [18] But one is crucified with Christ not because this way is demonstrably the way to life, but only because it is *revealed* to one as the way to life. And to presuppose a revealing act, to speak of " God " as " communicating," is to speak mythologically — " of the otherworldly in terms of this world, of the divine in terms of the human." Bultmann cannot avoid mythological presuppositions or mythological language. When he says, " He who endured death was already the Son of God," [19] he has certainly not demythologized. But further, one cannot speak of the love of God, or of the forgiveness of God without speaking mythologically. One cannot understand the crucifixion if the " divine " is not understood " in terms of the human."

Bultmann errs, however, not simply in believing that he has succeeded in demythologizing. He further impoverishes the gospel by interpreting the crucifixion only in terms of dying with Christ. Something must also be said about the justice, and the mercy, and the forgiveness of God that are also revealed, and about the sacrifice made on behalf of us all.

XII

The Resurrection

THE MEANING OF THE CROSS

In Chapter V we discussed various criticisms that have been brought against Bultmann's interpretation of the resurrection. In this chapter we shall defend certain aspects of Bultmann's interpretation, as well as show that in other significant respects he does not accurately represent the New Testament message.

The resurrection is for Bultmann neither a historical nor a mythical event. It is rather the interpretation in faith of the meaning of the cross. " To speak of the resurrection of Christ is nothing other than to express the meaning of the cross," [1] he writes; and " faith in the resurrection is nothing else than faith in the cross as the saving event." [2] When Bultmann refers to the resurrection as an " object of faith," [3] he is still not referring to it as a historical event but he is referring to the meaning of the crucifixion in which one believes.

Bultmann goes on to say that the resurrection cannot be a " proving miracle "; [4] that is, the meaning of the cross cannot be proved by citing the resurrection. He gives three reasons why this cannot be done:

1. It is unbelievable as a mythical event — as the return of a dead man to a bodily life.

197

2. The resurrection could not be confirmed by eye-witnesses so that on the basis of reports one could believe it.

3. " The resurrection is itself an object of faith, and one cannot prove one belief (belief in the saving meaning of the cross) by another belief (belief in the resurrection) ." [5]

In his first two reasons Bultmann uses the word " resurrection " in a sense that he has rejected. Indeed, he might as well have said that the resurrection cannot be a proving miracle because it is not a miracle — that is, a miraculous event. But in his third reason Bultmann has introduced a confusion by referring to belief in the resurrection as a *different* belief from belief in the cross as the saving event. He says that one cannot prove one belief by another, and the two beliefs to which he refers he has already said to be the same belief: " the resurrection . . . is the meaning of the cross." [6] He might better have said, it would seem, that one cannot prove the meaning of the cross by the resurrection because the resurrection *is* the meaning of the cross and a meaning cannot be proved simply by being repeated.

In his existential interpretation Bultmann has removed the " miraculous and the supernatural " from the resurrection and has interpreted it in accordance with what he believes to have been its original and permanent meaning. He has called the crucifixion and the resurrection a " unity," [7] and he has interpreted the resurrection as faith in the cross as saving event. This is the extent of his positive remarks about the resurrection. But does it agree with the New Testament, and if it does, is it sufficient?

Bultmann has called the cross and the resurrection a " unity "; but by " unity " he does not mean that they occurred simultaneously. For him, the cross was one event, and the Easter event was subsequent to it. According to Bultmann, the Easter event is not historical if it is understood as the resurrection of Christ, but only if it is understood as the beginning of the belief in the cross as the saving event. That is to say, the Easter event is historical if it is understood as the beginning of the belief in the resurrection; it is not historical if it is understood as referring to the resurrection as an event.

Now, this faith in the resurrection — the belief in the cross as the event of salvation — followed, chronologically, the crucifixion, and it is significant to point out that a space of time separated the two events. The interpretation of the meaning of the cross (the Easter faith, or the resurrection) was not given with the crucifixion, but followed it. This is true in the New Testament both with reference to the crucifixion of Jesus and the interpretation of it which followed, and with reference to Paul's application of these events to the lives of believers in terms of dying with Christ and living with him (Rom. 6:8, etc.). With regard to the latter concept, the life with Christ, or union with him in a resurrection like his, or the walking in newness of life, are always subsequent to the dying with Christ and the union with him in his death. Paul never refers to the two as taking place simultaneously, and the life always follows the death, the resurrection follows the burial. With regard to the death and resurrection of Jesus (or, in Bultmann's terms, the death and its interpretation) the latter is subsequent to the former and is never simultaneous with it.

It may seem that I have labored a very obvious point, but I have done so because Bultmann implies that *in reality* the crucifixion and the resurrection — the defeat and the victory — occurred simultaneously. He is aware that the disciples were not conscious of this, that their interpretation of the meaning of the cross succeeded the crucifixion itself. But he implies that the disciples were not aware of this meaning until after it had actually been given; that is, their Easter faith, their belief in the meaning of the cross, did not stem from any event other than the crucifixion itself, and it was therefore a delayed response that *could* have been made at the foot of the cross. The understanding of the meaning of the cross — the Easter faith — was revealed in the crucifixion, but was not understood until some time later. To corroborate this understanding, Bultmann refers to the Gospel of John, which " understands Jesus' exaltation in a double sense: as the exaltation on the cross and as the exaltation to Lordship." [8]

Is this interpretation of the resurrection in agreement with the New Testament record? I do not think so. Bultmann cites the Fourth Gospel in support of his view; but at no point in his gospel does John ever suggest that the resurrection was simply an interpretation of the crucifixion. It may be quite true that John may be interpreted as saying that Jesus' exaltation on the cross was also his exaltation to Lordship; but John also considered Jesus to have been exalted and glorified *before* his crucifixion (cf. John 13:31, etc.). Jesus, in the Fourth Gospel, is Lord not only on the cross, but throughout his whole earthly pilgrimage. Unless, then, most of John's Gospel, the Synoptic Gospels, Acts, Paul's letters, and all the other passages of the New Testament that refer to the resurrection of Christ are rejected, I do not see how one can accept Bultmann's identification of the defeat on Good Friday with the victory on Easter as in reality simultaneous events, or one event. The fact that the interpretation of the meaning of the cross was not given or recognized until *after* the event of the cross, according to every witness of the New Testament, and the fact that this same interpretation was arrived at by several disciples independently of each other and apparently at about the same time, would suggest that another event had intervened between the crucifixion and the interpretation of its meaning.

BELIEF AND INTERPRETATION

What led to this interpretation of the cross as the event of salvation? There was nothing extraordinary in crucifixions; nor was there anything unique in the martyrdom of a leader for a great cause or a great faith. Moreover, the gospel accounts record loneliness, bewilderment, and great disappointment after Jesus' crucifixion; and not even the report of the empty tomb changed this (although here we undoubtedly have a mingling of traditions). Yet this whole attitude *was* changed. What brought about this reversal, this interpretation? Bultmann's theory would be much more tenable if the records indicated that the interpretation was arrived at by one disciple who explained it to others, who in turn explained it further. But the records indicate quite a different situation: (*a*) that the resurrection was believed in independently by several disciples; (*b*) that the interpretation of the meaning of the crucifixion as the saving event was not given until *after* a prior statement was made about an event subsequent to the crucifixion — namely, the resurrection. It was only after this event took place that an interpretation of the meaning of the cross was gradually undertaken and developed.

It is significant that in the whole of Peter's sermon in the second chapter of Acts there is not one reference to the meaning of the cross. An existential interpretation of the crucifixion's meaning was, of course, derived and worked out later; but what was preached *first* was not a new understanding of existence revealed in the crucifixion, but an act of God in history. Peter did not even promise that as Christ was raised from the dead so also would those who believed in him be raised. He says only that Christ was raised. The implications of this were to follow. It is difficult to account for this situation if one describes the resurrection faith simply as the understanding of the meaning of the cross. This was not the original resurrection faith which in the beginning had nothing directly to do with the crucifixion or its interpretation, but was a statement of faith regarding a subsequent event.

And finally, the records indicate that, not only was an event preached (the resurrection) and a new understanding of life given, but, in addition, a new power was given, and this, also, at the very beginning. The history of Stoicism reveals that a noble philosophy of life is not sufficient to live by; to the disciples was given not only a new philosophy, a new understanding of the way in which life is fulfilled, but also a new power by which to live. The history of the early church, read even disinterestedly, reveals a new dynamic in the lives of Christians that the Romans had never known. There was something more in the church than a new understanding of life; there was power — the power that Peter promised after his early sermon: " You shall receive the gift of the Holy Spirit " (Acts 2:38) . Bultmann has failed to report the new power as he has failed to account adequately for the new understanding; and this is an unavoidable consequence of his demythologization. For to speak of the *cause* of an interpretation of the cross as saving event, and to speak of the new power that was given, is to speak mythologically of the entrance of the supernatural into the realm of the natural, of the divine into the realm of the human.

Bultmann is not able to appropriate or to demythologize the concept of the Spirit. He defines the Spirit as the "genuine possibility of a new life which must be appropriated by deliberate resolve"; [9] and then he is satisfied that "the concept of the 'Spirit' is thus demythologized" [10] — i.e., freed from mythology. The Spirit, however, has not been demythologized unless in the process it has become exclusively a matter of "resolve." To "appropriate" the "new life," it must be offered; and the offering is not a matter of resolve, but of an activity of God in the direction of and on behalf of man. To speak of such an activity, however, to speak of the "appropriation" of a gift, is necessarily to speak mythologically. So Bultmann is not able to say anything about the Spirit that is given in the church.

Although I consider Bultmann's treatment of the resurrection to be inadequate, I must also defend him in the following points:

1. Bultmann is right in understanding the crucifixion and the resurrection as a unity; and the resurrection is, in part at least, faith in the cross as the event of salvation. But one must not forget that the crucifixion and the resurrection also have independent meanings and do not constitute one event plus an interpretation.

2. Bultmann is also right, I believe, in denying that the resurrection is a historical event. The resurrection cannot be understood as a purely historical event because it is known only by revelation as it was known on the first Easter only by those to whom it was revealed. Historical events lend themselves to empirical validation; the resurrection does not so lend itself. As revelation, it is not and

never has been provable. It has always been a tenet of
faith and never a demonstrable occurrence. It was an understanding and an experience that, known only by revelation, could be described only in the language of myth.
This language was later historified. In the return of the
crucified Lord to those who had known him in the flesh
came a new understanding of the nature and will of God,
of the meaning and destiny of life, as well as a new power
to undergird life. But the return of Christ could not be
described except in the dramatic language of image and
myth. The church, then, very soon interpreted this language literally, as it has done to the present day. But if
the resurrection experiences happened just as they are described in many passages in the Gospels, they could not
have been known as revelation, and they could have been
known by others than those to whom they were revealed.
Christ's resurrection would have been demonstrable, and
therefore not revelation; for it is always the nature of revelation that it cannot be proved but can be received only by
faith. It must be freely decided for.

But Bultmann's interpretation of the resurrection fails
in the following respects:

1. In implying that the meaning of the cross was given
in the crucifixion itself, it fails to account for the fact that
this meaning was not seen at the cross, but later, and by
various persons independent of each other.

2. It does not account for the referend to which an existentially understood "rising with Christ" corresponds.
There is only the referend in the crucifixion to the "dying
with Christ." We cannot be "raised with Christ" if Christ
was not raised. If the resurrection faith is the understanding of the meaning of the crucifixion and not the response
to a post-crucifixion event, then to be raised with Christ

has no analogy in the experience of Christ. Bultmann knows only of the dying of Christ and of the response of believers; but Paul speaks of two events, not one. Paul understood the resurrection as an event, just as he did the crucifixion; he could therefore speak of being raised with Christ as well as of dying with Christ. If Christ was not raised, no future *was* in actuality opened to *him,* and the future opened to the Christian who dies with Christ becomes only an illusion. This concept, upon which Bultmann leans so heavily in his interpretation of the meaning of the Christ-event, can have little meaning unless it corresponds to two events experienced by the disciples.

3. In interpreting the resurrection as showing the meaning of life as revealed in the crucifixion, Bultmann fails to account for the early preaching that proclaimed, not a new understanding of existence, but a recent act of God that was only later to be interpreted existentially.

4. In his interpretation of the resurrection Bultmann does not account for the new power that the records indicate was given to believers.

5. In his discussion of the meaning of the resurrection, Bultmann does not sufficiently emphasize the promise of the final resurrection after death which is given to believers.

6. Finally, the New Testament knows of a witness to the validity of the Christian faith. According to Bultmann, a man believes the faith because it is preached to him as believable. He answers either yes or no. But Bultmann knows of no verification of faith. If the believer says, " Yes," that to which he assents is never confirmed. The New Testament, on the other hand, knows of a confirmation from heaven, of a witness who verifies the believer's faith. This witness is none other than God himself, in the Holy Spirit;

for " the Spirit is the witness " (I John 5:7 ff.). Christians are not forced to rely simply on their own judgment, to cast their lives here rather than there, because this seems truer than that. Paul did not rejoice in prison and consider it better to die and be with Christ than to live with him simply because it was preached to him that way. No, what was preached to Paul had been verified by God, for Paul had "received the Holy Spirit." Again turning to Peter's sermon, we read that the gift of the Holy Spirit was promised to those who were baptized (Acts 2:38). Peter himself received it, and so did not deny his Lord a second time. We know, not only from Peter and Paul, but also from " ten thousand times ten thousand " that this promise was vouchsafed. In his interpretation of the resurrection, Bultmann omits to account for the presence of Christ in his church, and the power and verification that are thereby given. This presence is more than an aid to understanding. It enlightens, to be sure, but it also confirms and sustains.

XIII

The Authority of the Bible

THE DETERMINATION OF AUTHORITY

I should like finally to consider the question of the authority of the Bible, with particular reference to the New Testament. But before we speak of the Bible at all, we must remember that the Christian's final and absolute authority is God as he is revealed in Jesus Christ. No statement regarding the authority of Scripture can be allowed in any way to contradict this. The authority of the Bible must be related to the authority of God in Christ.

Two questions now face us. First: Is the Bible authoritative? Second: If it is, in what sense is it authoritative? These two questions are closely related to each other, and the answer given to each depends to a degree upon the answer given to the other. It is not only true that the sense in which the Bible is authoritative cannot be determined until the question of whether the Bible is authoritative at all is answered, but it is also true that the answer to the question as to whether the Bible is authoritative depends upon the meaning given to the word " authoritative," that is, upon the sense in which the question is asked. Although, then, the answer to each question depends in part upon the answer given to the other, clarity requires us to deal with the questions successively.

Let us turn then to the first question. Is the Bible au-

thoritative? That is to say, does it in any respect say the
last word to the Christian? Is the Bible uniquely authoritative in the sense that it is finally normative, that it judges
all and is judged by none? There are many powers in the
world, and there are many faiths declared to be true. The
question is not, Does the Bible contain some truth, some
measure of authority? — for none could deny that it does.
The question rather is, Is the Bible absolutely and finally
authoritative and normative for all other authority? To
answer this question let us begin by turning our memories
back to the first decades and centuries of the Christian
church, when the New Testament canon was being formulated.

The first Christians — the first men who believed that
Jesus had been raised from the dead and who called him
Lord — were Jews, for whom the Old Testament constituted the oracles of God. For Jews of the first century it
was " an uncontested axiom that every syllable of Scripture " (that is, the Old Testament) " had the verity and
authority of the Word of God." [1] Every word of Scripture
was believed to be of divine origin and authority, having
been communicated by God either directly (as in Moses'
case) or through dreams and visions, or through the in-
spiration of the spirit. And the early Christians ascribed
no less authority to the Old Testament than did the Jews.
More than that, it was the Old Testament that supplied
the Christians with proof of their claims with regard to
Christ. The Old Testament was in the early church quite
literally the Word of God, inspired in all its parts, con-
taining no errors and no contradictions. The Old Testament canon had, for the most part, been set; and was not
to be enlarged, especially by books that were known to
have been written since the days of the last prophets fol-

lowing whom the spirit was believed to have departed from Israel.

But the first Christians had, in addition to their Old Testament Scriptures, the words of their Lord Jesus; and their minds were full of memories of him who had taught them with authority, who had so recently suffered many things, whom they had forsaken, who had been crucified, and who miraculously had appeared to them on the third day. His words were as authoritative as the words of Moses and of the prophets. The Spirit that had departed with the prophets had returned to Jesus at his baptism, so that he had spoken with an authority equal to theirs. More than that, the Holy Spirit had descended upon the Christians as Joel had foretold would occur in the last days. Their message was that the promises of the Old Testament whose fulfilling had been long awaited in Israel, were now accomplished. Jesus, who had been crucified, was the Messiah. What he had said, what he had done, what had happened to him, was the completion of God's revelation of himself and of his purpose for man. None of this had been accidental — not even the crucifixion; it was all of it the end toward which the Old Testament pointed. All could share in this fulfillment if they would but " repent, and be baptized . . . in the name of Jesus Christ " (Acts 2:38).

Quite naturally and unconsciously, the fulfillment of the Old Testament Scriptures was preached together with the promises of those Scriptures. The promises could not any longer be preached alone; indeed, the emphasis could not even lie on them. The emphasis must now lie on the fulfillment, with the promises preached in order that what was fulfilled might be understood.

From the moment, then, at which Jesus was first

preached as Messiah, as the fulfillment of Old Testament expectations, an addition had been made to Old Testament authority. The Old Testament, to those who received Jesus as Messiah, no longer comprised the whole of God's revelation to Israel. The revelation had now been extended in the revealing of its climax. There was as yet no new canon — nothing had been written down. But there was already the antecedent of a canon — the words of the Messiah, the story about him, and the understanding that was being formulated of precisely what God had said and done " in these last days." And although all this was in oral form, it was no less authoritative. Jesus' words were repeated, not simply as words of an honored teacher, but as words of the Messiah. His acts were likewise remembered as acts that had been performed by the Messiah.

And still more important — but so very hard to penetrate — the meaning of it all, what God had said in and through his Messiah, must be proclaimed! Those who had witnessed and accepted Jesus as Messiah formed a new community, the church. This was a preaching community. Christ had not commanded the apostles to write, but to preach; and what we know as the church would have died with the first disciples had not this message been preached. As Paul wrote to the Romans: " How are men to call upon him in whom they have not believed? And how are they to believe in him of whom they have never heard? And how are they to hear without a preacher? " (Rom. 10:14.) Of course they could not! And so the preaching of the gospel led to the extension of the community. Where the gospel was preached, there the church sprang up. Could the church exist without this message? Quite clearly, no. Once the revelation had been given and responded to, the church came into being; and it was when this revelation

was preached that the community spread, the church
emerging almost overnight throughout the Mediterranean
world.

It is not our purpose to trace the subsequent history of
this kerygma, nor the ways in which the response to the
revelation was articulated. But the response was written
down, the writing representing a transitional stage of the
proclamation from an oral to a written form. No new authority accrued to the gospel as a result of this transition.
Jesus' words were no more authoritative if read from
papyrus than if quoted from memory, and surely Paul's
letters carried no more weight in the communities to
which he wrote than did his oral speech. No, the gospel in
written form was simply the means of bridging the gaps
of space and time. By this means Paul could exert his
apostolic authority from one end of the Mediterranean to
the other, and from the first century to the twentieth, and
on to the end. The New Testament preserves the apostolic
gospel and projects this gospel down through the ages until the Last Day.

Later, when the outside world attacked the church and,
still more serious, when dissensions arose within, the
apostles' written word was appealed to as final and authoritative. No influential bishops and no church council de-
creed this literature to be authoritative. It simply was by
virtue of the fact that it had grown out of the church, that
it represented the consensus held by Christ's original
apostles, that it was the written account, formulated by
the community as a whole, of what God had done in
Christ. No one apostle had formulated this gospel, and no
one cleric could alter it; nor could the community as a
whole do so. To what other source could the church have
turned? Here was recorded the heart of the church's mes-

sage. Quite naturally Christians quoted from these books without preface or comment, not rendering an independent opinion with regard to them but, as Westcott said, following " an unquestioned judgment." [2]

The mind of the church as a whole had settled by common usage on a group of writings as authoritative long before any church councils were held. The church did not need consciously to decide that it would add a group of writings to the Old Testament; before the church knew it, it had already done so. To quote Westcott again, " With the exception of the epistle to the Hebrews, the two shorter epistles of St. John, the second epistle of St. Peter, the epistles of St. James and St. Jude, and the Apocalypse " — seven of our twenty-seven New Testament books, and three of which are of little consequence — " all the other books of the New Testament are acknowledged as apostolic and authoritative throughout the church at the close of the second century." [3] " Slow experience and spiritual instinct decided the practical judgment of the church. . . . Without controversy and without effort ' the gospel and the apostles ' were recognized as inspired sources of truth in the same sense as ' the Law and the Prophets.' " [4]

As far as the seven books are concerned, they were not universally known. But we are not here concerned with the third-, fourth-, and fifth-century question of precisely which books were to make up the New Testament canon. We wish only to emphasize that the authority of what we might call the heart of our New Testament was never disputed in the early church. The authority of the message that these books proclaim did not rest upon a decision of the church that might later have been called into question. No, the message witnessed to in these books was the message that had called into being the Christian communities of the Roman Empire. For these communities to question the proclamation of faith that they had received in its written form would have been for them to question the witness they were making in the world and to question the new foundation upon which their lives had been set and in devotion to which not a few had sacrificed themselves in the arena.

The basic message of the church, the core of its proclamation, has always been the message proclaimed in the New Testament. The Bible is not only authoritative for the church; the church cannot be itself without the Bible. For the church to question the authority of Scripture is not simply for it to question the authority of a document, external to itself, which it may accept or dispose of as it will. Rather it questions its own authority, whether it be of man or of God. For the church to question the authority of Scripture is for it to question the validity of its message and of its historic function in the world. The church and the Bible are inseparable. Each brought into being and embraced the other, and one without the other would die.

The Bible is and must remain in some sense the final authority in the church, and without the Bible the church cannot be the church. The Bible is the stage from which Christ speaks, and from that stage he exerts his authority over his church. But this authority is not to be considered different in kind from the authority that Christ exercised over his disciples in first-century Palestine. Then, we are told, he taught as one having authority. What kind of authority? Not that of a demagogue exerted powerfully over his followers to the extent that their freedom became his prerogative. Peter was free to deny, Judas to betray. Then wherein lay Christ's authority? It lay here, that his reference was not to man but to God. He taught and acted by no standard other than the will of God. He was authoritative, then, only over the lives of those who identified the source of his authority and who subjected themselves to the same authority. Christ did not impose his authority over men, to be accepted uncritically, without inner endorsement and apart from a free decision of the will. On the contrary, having proclaimed the will and the judgments and the promises of God, he was delivered over to be crucified. Here was no despot; here was the Lamb of God that was slain.

The authority of the Bible is not different in kind from that exercised by Jesus. It is not tyrannical in character; it does not overrule man's freedom; it is not imposed upon man from the outside to be accepted whether or not it validates itself as true — and any church that tries such an imposition does not understand wherein the power of the Bible lies. It is rather an authority that must be decided for and accepted in faith as from God. And to deny it is to deny Christ.

THE CANON AND AUTHORITY

We have seen that the kerygma of the church, the basic Christian teaching and preaching, was not a matter to be decided by church assemblies and ecclesiastical councils, but was inherited by the church from the first disciples and apostles. The kerygma is related dialectically to the church; neither exists without the other. By the middle of the second century the direction that this message was to take had been established by common usage. Trinitarian and Christological problems were settled by councils; but in these discussions Scripture was assumed to be normative, and even heretics used the Bible to argue their heresies.

Although, then, it is true to say that the Christian proclamation was not decided by edicts or councils but by general use, this cannot be said of the canon. It was inevitable
that some books would be known and used in one part of
the church and not in another. And so it was that lists of
canonical books, which were drawn up in various Christian centers by different church leaders, were not identical; but during the third, fourth, and fifth centuries, the
twenty-seven books that constitute our New Testament,
together with the Old Testament, became canon.

Yet it would not do to overemphasize the differences in
these early lists of books. They were, in fact, strikingly
similar. As Westcott has written: " Briefly it may be said
that wherever the East and the West entered into a true
union " (for example, at Alexandria and Caesarea) " there
the canon is found perfect, while the absence or incom-
pleteness of this union is the measure of the corresponding
defects in the canon." [5] Only the Apocalypse was a subject
of much controversy, and that largely because of the mis-
use made of it by the Montanists.

The conciliar canons wrought no new work; the canon
had in fact already come into being without any authoritative decision behind it. The canon of Eusebius was much
like our own, although Eusebius was not quite sure
whether the Apocalypse should be included. Later Atha-
nasius issued a list of authoritative books that included
the Apocalypse and was in all other respects like that of
Eusebius, and the question of the canon was practically
settled. When Jerome and Augustine independently sup-
ported the same canon, and the list of Pope Gelasius confirmed the books of the New Testament that we now receive to be canonical, the New Testament was fixed.

The canon was, then, a matter of some dispute, as the

basic gospel message was not. And the question arises, in
discussing the authority of the Bible, as to whether it is
the canon that is to be authoritative, or a part of the canon,
and if a part, then what part? There have been those who
have accepted the authority of parts of the canon while
rejecting the authority of the whole. Some books have
been held to contain the gospel in its purest form, while
others have been held inferior. Martin Luther made such
a distinction within the canon. He found a gospel within
the gospel, and judged the books of the New Testament
according to their witness to Christ. His selection of some
New Testament books that reveal Christ and teach what
is needful and blessed to know, and his relegation of other
books to a lower realm as inferior, was based on his an-
terior conception of what constituted the gospel. Thus
Luther, in judging the sources of Christian doctrine, also
passed judgment on Christian doctrine itself.

Inevitably, any Christian will find that parts of the New
Testament speak to him more plainly than others, that
some portions represent and preach Christ more clearly
than others, that some books seem to be the epitome of the
gospel, while others deal with secondary considerations.
And it is this fact which, among others, accounts for the
differences to be found among various theological statements and points of view. But such a judgment should not
be made an article of faith to be imposed on the church as
a whole. Any such judgment must inevitably be in part subjective. Luther, to be sure, appealed to external standards
when he stated that such books as Hebrews, James, and the
Apocalypse were not truly and certainly " capital books "
of the New Testament. He doubted that any one of them
had been written by an apostle, and historical criticism has
tended to bear him out. But many historical critics are also
of the opinion that the Fourth Gospel was not written by

an "apostle" either, the Gospel that Luther cherished above all. Yet historical tests were not decisive for Luther, for he also wrote that no book that did not teach Christ was apostolic, even if it had been written by an apostle, and that any book that preaches Christ is apostolic "even if Judas, Annas, Pilate, and Herod preached it." [6] Luther's final test was not historical, but subjective and personal. He asked, Does this book preach Christ to me?

That a Christian should ask such a question of Biblical books is altogether natural and right. Luther cannot be judged for having asked this question. But the church cannot accept either his judgment or that of any Christian as to which books preach Christ when throughout the centuries different books have validated themselves to different Christians as peculiarly authentic. It would be an error to absolutize the judgment of any theologian, or even of any group of Christians, as to which books in the New Testament canon preach Christ. The Bible is first of all the church's book before it is my book, or any one else's book, and there is always a tension between the Bible as the church's book and the Bible as my book.

Although it is true that only those parts of the New Testament which authenticate themselves to me as true can be authoritative for me, it is also true that the whole of the Bible is normative for the whole of the church in whose context alone I can understand it. Tension arises out of the fact that a part of the New Testament validates itself to me, while the whole of the New Testament is normative for the Christian community to which I belong and from which I have received the gospel. I must always, therefore, reapproach the whole New Testament in the attempt to broaden my understanding of the gospel that the church preaches as apostolic.

Every man builds his own theology partly on the basis

of his understanding of Scripture, and differences in theology are largely to be accounted for on the basis of differences in understanding of the Bible. But no theologian can stand in absolute judgment of Scripture because of his particular response to it, for it is Scripture that stands in judgment of every theologian, and must continue to do so if the church is to remain the church. The Bible cannot be clipped to fit any theology. The peeling off of layers has been tried before — from Marcion on down through the centuries — but the gospel in its fullness will not be cut down. It is still preached, and will be preached. By the grace of God we have recorded in the New Testament a diversity of response to the Word of God incarnate. The New Testament does not present us with one clear-cut, unambiguous point of view. It is rather a cluster of many precious jewels, no one of which dare be removed, least of all that stone which most severely judges a man.

The canon, however, can be accepted only in faith. It is a collection of apostolic writings, which in faith are self-validating, and many come from East and West to take from it treasures new and old. That some parts of it should speak with clearer voice than other parts has always been true, and will continue to be true. But no man's response to it can be finally authoritative except for that man. Each must read with his own eyes and hear with his own ears and receive for himself what God will say to him.

Yet the canon is not authoritative in a magical sense. It is not inconceivable that it should have been different from what it is. The New Testament, for example, might well have contained twenty-four or twenty-five, twenty-nine or thirty, books instead of twenty-seven. The books that make up our Bible are not in themselves holy things. They are not holy and they are not authoritative until they come alive. It is *God's* Word that is holy and authoritative; and *God's* Word does not lie on a shelf, and is not dusted when the house is cleaned. When the sacred Christian writings are referred to as " The New Covenant," it must be remembered that the books so-called are, more precisely, the *record* or *account* of the New Covenant, and do not constitute the *terms* of the New Covenant. To understand " New Covenant " in the latter sense leads to the erroneous identification of God's Word with the words of Scripture. Christ is the Word of God, and in and through Christ God made the New Covenant with all who will believe. This Covenant is recorded in the books we call " The New Testament " (cf. I Cor. 11:25; II Cor. 3:4-6; Mark 14:24).

THE BIBLE AND THE WORD OF GOD

When the Bible is read or preached, an event takes place to which one must respond. When this event occurs the words of Scripture convey the Word of God, and it is this Word which, coming alive, is authoritative. But the Word of God does not come alive, does not appear, is not heard, except in a dialogue. The words of the Bible remain dead unless a person converses with them. He must come to the Bible with a question if he is to hear the Word of God. He may come boasting and ask for justification, or he may come anxious and ask for guidance, or he may come beseeching and ask a blessing. But whatever his question, he must come with his whole life and his whole self and be prepared to bring all his faculties into a dialogue.

The preacher must also hold a dialogue with Scripture. Exposition is always done from man's side, and never from God's side. And if the congregation is to profit by the sermon, it must engage in this dialogue with the preacher. But whatever the dialogue, and wherever it is carried on, it is only when a dialogue is held with the Bible that its words, otherwise dead, come alive and confront man with the holy Word of God.

Something further must now be said about the way in which the Word of God is related to the words of Scripture. It is clear that God's Word is mediated through words of men, and that we cannot know the Word of God except through the words of witnesses who mediate it. We confront here a paradoxical situation. On the one hand, the words of Scripture cannot be equated with the Word of God; but on the other hand, it is primarily and uniquely through the words of Scripture that we know the Word of God. Orthodoxy has tended to make too small a distinction between the Word of God and the words of Scripture; liberalism has tended to make too great a distinction between the Word of God and the words of Scripture. At both extremes the meaning of Scripture is limited: in orthodoxy by a literalism that crushes out the possibility of fresh insight; in liberalism by the removal of " layers " of Scripture to the point where, on occasion, what has remained has been little more than a vapor. But both extremes are in error. On the one hand, the Word of God cannot be completely abstracted and separated from the words of Scripture.[7] The Word of God does not come to a man unmediated.

Dr. Albert Peel in an essay on " Protestant Views of the Authority of the Bible " quotes R. W. Dale as saying: " Practically, the Bible does not come between me and God. . . . The book — explain it how we may — vanishes. The truth read there shines in its own light." [8] This view is intriguing, and one has a certain sympathy with it; but it does not solve the problem of the authority of Scripture as Dale appears to assume. Because, however much a man may feel that the book vanishes, in point of fact, so long as he is reading it, the book does not vanish. And however much he may forget the authors whose works he is reading — as Dale says he does — he is still reading words that have sifted through or been created in the minds of particular men. To hear the Word of God in Scripture is not *just* to hear the Word of God; it is also to hear Scripture. This is inevitable.

We must not, then, identify revelation with the medium that has received and recorded it; those who witnessed and recorded the revelation were not themselves equal in authority to the Revealer. Not even Paul was infallible, as he himself was quite aware. The Biblical record, therefore, reflects different degrees as well as different kinds of comprehension and understanding. Not all Biblical writings are on the same level of insight, nor do they all say the same thing. Although revelation depends on what God reveals, it is meaningless apart from what man understands. And man's comprehension depends on two factors: the gifts that God has given, and the use that man has made of such gifts up to the point of the revelation. There is, then, a contingent element involved in the reception of revelation, derived from varieties of gifts and from human freedom, and this element is reflected in the New Testament.

But granted the element of contingency involved, the situation still remains that we cannot hear the gospel except as it has been mediated to us by the apostles. A man who has never seen or heard of the Bible, or of any literature dependent on the Bible, could hardly expound the Word of God as known in Jesus Christ. Who but a reader of the Bible could ever know that while we were yet sinners Christ died for us and that on the third day he was raised from the dead? This Word of God is communicated to us only through Scripture and exposition of Scripture. I can, of course, commune with God apart from reading Scripture; but I as a Christian know the God with whom I commune only because I have read Scripture.

Another factor involved concerns the mythological framework in which the New Testament kerygma is set, as well as the mythological character of a great deal of the content of the New Testament. If it is true that only the language of myth can convey the content of myth, and that a myth and its object become so intermingled that what the myth says cannot be precisely said in any other language, then from this point of view also the Word of God as recorded in the New Testament is ultimately inseparable from the language and the thought forms of the New Testament.

Furthermore, I cannot get behind Scripture to God as he is revealed in Jesus Christ. I can know God through Jesus Christ only from *this* side of the Bible. The theologian, then, must engage in exegesis. He cannot get behind the Bible to the revelation witnessed to in the Bible; he can only believe in the revelation as he lets the Bible speak to him of it. The final and authoritative Word of God is mediated through words of the Bible and cannot be heard except through those words.

But on the other side of the paradox it is equally true that the words of the Bible cannot be equated with the Word of God, for the Word of God in the Bible is the thought, intention, will, or deed of God, revealed finally in his Son, Jesus Christ. It is not a means of communicating thought through vibrations of the vocal cords. To accept the Bible as the *words* of God would not be to understand either revelation or God as the Bible understands them. Moreover, so to understand the Bible as God's words

would be not only to engage in an intolerably literal an-
thropomorphism, but also to involve God in contradictions, and in scientific and historical errors, not to mention
occasional bad grammar. To understand the words of the
Bible as the Word of God leaves a man in an impossible
situation when his own experience points to one conclusion while his external authority leads to another. To affirm his experience he must deny his authority; to affirm
his authority he must move in an imaginary world that
God has not created and where His voice is not heard. The
Bible is then, in the interests of a theory *about* it, not allowed to speak. Clearly, in the early church the exact words
in which the tradition was formulated were handled with
considerable freedom. (For demonstration of this consult
any harmony of the Synoptic Gospels.) The writers of the
Gospels certainly did not believe that the words they used
were identical with God's Word, nor did any New Testament author. " Thus saith the Lord " can never simply
mean " Thus do I write with pen and ink! "

But if it be true that the Biblical authors are not themselves revealers, but are rather the recorders of revelation,
is it not the case that in Christ we confront a quite different situation? For Christ was not a recorder of revelation,
but was himself the revealer of God. Then are not the
words of Christ in a somewhat different category from the
words of those who witnessed to Christ? If we cannot take
any other words of Scripture as revelation, must we not at
least so understand the words that are recorded as spoken
by Jesus?

To answer this question involves us, in the first place, in
a critical problem, a problem that arises as a result of historical investigations. There is not complete agreement in
the Gospels as to just what Jesus said. It is generally as-

sumed by modern critics that the Fourth Gospel cannot as a rule be held to contain Jesus' actual words. And when Matthew, Mark, and Luke are compared there are many discrepancies in the words that Jesus is recorded to have spoken. For example, all three of these Gospels record Peter's confession of Jesus' Messiahship at Caesarea Philippi, but only Matthew records that Jesus replied to Peter, " You are Peter, and on this rock I will build my church." Aside from the meaning of these famous words, which is not certain, the further question remains as to whether Jesus said them at all, and if he did, whether he said them in this or in some other context. Many other examples could be given. The situation is that Jesus' exact words cannot be determined with any finality. Historical and literary criticism can detect but cannot reconcile the differences; and on the basis of evidence now available, in many instances precisely what Jesus said, and the context in which he said it, simply cannot be known with assurance.

In the second place, we have Jesus' words recorded only in translation. If Jesus knew the Greek language at all — and there is no evidence either that he did or that he did not — the probability is that he taught his disciples in Aramaic. If this *was* the language that he used, then we know his teachings only in translation — translation from a Semitic to an Indo-European language. Exact meanings are frequently difficult or impossible to recapture in translating from one Indo-European language to another where the root words are often the same. But the problem is greatly increased in translating from a non-Indo-European to an Indo-European language. This means that even if the Gospels agreed in their accounts of Jesus' words, which they do not, we would still have reason to question whether or not Jesus' intention had been accurately recorded.

Finally, there is a third difficulty. There are a few words, accorded to Jesus in the Gospels, that are simply not true. For example: In Mark, ch. 13, Jesus is quoted as referring to wars, earthquakes, famines, the darkening of the sun, and moon, the stars falling from heaven, the Son of Man coming in clouds, and the gathering of the elect. And Jesus concludes: " Truly, I say to you, this generation will not pass away before all these things take place." But even the most ingenious believer cannot show that anything resembling these events took place before the generation of Jesus had passed away.

There are four possibilities open to the exegete of this passage: either Jesus was here in error, or he never said these words at all, or he said them, but they do not mean what they say, or his words were misunderstood and do not faithfully report his meaning. But in any case — unless one accepts the third possibility, which leads to totally irresponsible exegesis — it cannot be held that Jesus' words as we have them in the Gospels are infallible. To say that Jesus' words are infallible would have to mean not his words as we possess them, but a selection from them, or most of them, but not all of them. Or it would have to mean that Jesus' words do not mean what Jesus meant to say, in which case we would have to admit that we could never know what Jesus' intention had been, and the infallibility of an enigma is not much help. If we made a selection of Jesus' words that we held to be infallible, we would not be accepting a word of Jesus as authoritative because it is reported as a word of Jesus, but because it commends itself to us as a word of Jesus — the criterion thus becoming not the Gospel record, but our own subjective judgment.

To return, then, to the question that we asked: If we cannot accept any other Scriptural words as infallible, must we not at least accept Jesus' words as such? The answer must be no, because we cannot know exactly what Jesus said and because some words that are attributed to him are in error, but most importantly because it is Christ who is the revealer, who is authoritative, and not his words.

In conclusion, let us repeat that the Word of God must be authoritative in the church, the Word of God to which the Bible bears witness. This is a living Word, inseparable from the Bible but never to be identified with the Bible. The question as to the nature of the authority of the Bible cannot be settled at any time with finality. This is a question that the church must always ask of itself, the answer to which will vary from age to age; for the answer must always be related to the results of historical inquiry, and to hermeneutical method. It is inconceivable, for example, that the church of the sixteenth century, reborn to a lively faith as it was, could possibly have determined the manner in which the Bible was to be considered authoritative in the twentieth century. If, in the providence of God, the great reformers had agreed in their understanding of the authority of Scripture, their agreement would still have represented the mind only of the church of their day, and could not have been binding on another day. And we cannot hope, we dare not presume to issue a final decree, valid for the ages. Biblical critics, theologians, and all Christians together, in conversations with each other, must ever seek new insight, relevant to their own day, into the mysterious way in which the dumb are led to speak, the maimed to be whole, the lame to walk, and the blind to see, when they hear the Holy Word and can do no other than glorify the God of Israel and the Father of our Lord Jesus Christ.

Notes

CHAPTER I

1. The sense in which the Bible mediates the Word of God will be discussed in Chapter XIII.

CHAPTER II

1. Rudolf Bultmann, " Neues Testament und Mythologie: Das Problem der Entmythologisierung der neutestamentlichen Verkündigung," in *Kerygma und Mythos I,* ed. by Hans Werner Bartsch (Herbert Reich, Hamburg-Volksdorf, 1948), pp. 15–53. (Eng. tr., *Kerygma and Myth.*) Used by permission of the publisher, Herbert Reich.

2. *Ibid.,* p. 15.

3. *Ibid.,* p. 16.

4. *Ibid.,* p. 19.

5. *Ibid.,* p. 20.

6. *Ibid.,* p. 23, n. 2.

7. *Ibid.,* p. 23.

8. *Ibid.,* p. 26.

CHAPTER III

1. Bultmann, *loc. cit.,* p. 41.

2. *Ibid.,* p. 42.

3. I John 4:10, in Bultmann, *loc. cit.,* p. 43.

4. I John 4:19. Whole quotation from Bultmann, *loc. cit.,* pp. 42–43. Cf. Rom. 8:32; John 3:16; Gal. 1:4; 2:19 f.

5. Bultmann, *loc. cit.,* p. 43.

6. Wilhelm Kamlah, *Christentum und Selbstbehauptung* (1940), p. 353, cited by Bultmann, *loc. cit.,* p. 44.

7. Bultmann, *loc. cit.*, p. 44.

8. *Ibid.*, p. 45.

9. *Ibid.*, p. 46.

10. *Ibid.*, p. 47.

11. *Ibid.*

12. *Ibid.*, pp. 47 f.

13. *Ibid.*, p. 48.

14. Bultmann, "Karl Barth, 'Die Auferstehung der To-ten,'" in *Glauben und Verstehen* (J. C. B. Mohr, Tübingen, 1933), p. 54.

15. *Ibid.*, p. 55.

16. Bultmann, "Neues Testament und Mythologie," p. 50.

17. *Ibid.*

18. *Ibid.*

19. *Ibid.*, p. 51.

20. *Ibid.*

21. *Ibid.*

22. Rom. 10:17, from Bultmann, *ibid.*

23. Bultmann, "Neues Testament und Mythologie," p. 52.

24. *Ibid.*

25. *Ibid.*

Chapter IV

1. Julius Schniewind, "Antwort an Rudolf Bultmann," in *Kerygma und Mythos*, p. 110.

2. *Ibid.*, p. 103.

3. Bultmann, "Neues Testament und Mythologie," p. 47.

4. Schniewind, *loc. cit.*, p. 103.

5. *Ibid.*, p. 90.

6. Helmut Thielicke, "Die Frage der Entmythologisie-rung des Neuen Testaments," in *Kerygma und Mythos*, p. 186.

7. *Ibid.*, p. 185.

8. *Ibid.*

9. Schniewind, *loc. cit.*, p. 115.

10. *Ibid.*

11. *Ibid.*

12. Bultmann, "Zu J. Schniewinds Thesen," in *Kerygma und Mythos*, p. 142.

13. *Ibid.*

14. Bultmann, *Jesus and the Word* (Eng. tr., Charles Scribner's Sons, 1934).

15. Bultmann, " Neues Testament und Mythologie," p. 47.

16. *Ibid.*

17. Bultmann, " Zu J. Schniewinds Thesen," p. 143.

18. *Ibid.,* p. 142.

19. *Ibid.,* p. 143.

20. *Ibid.,* p. 146.

CHAPTER V

1. Cf. Bultmann, " Neues Testament und Mythologie," pp. 47–52.

2. Thielicke, *loc. cit.,* p. 191.

3. *Ibid.*

4. *Ibid.*

5. Schniewind, *loc. cit.,* p. 109.

6. *Ibid.,* p. 108. Cf. Rom. 4:5; Mark 9:24.

7. Bultmann, " Zu J. Schniewinds Thesen," p. 144.

8. Schniewind, *loc. cit.,* p. 108.

9. Paul Althaus, *Die christliche Wahrheit* (2d ed.; C. Bertelsmann, Gütersloh, 1949), Vol. II, p. 273.

10. *Ibid.*

11. Hermann Sasse, " Flucht vor dem Dogma," in *Luthertum* (1942), pp. 161 ff.

12. Markus Barth, *Der Augenzeuge* (A. G. Zollikon, Zürich, 1946), pp. 255 ff.

13. W. G. Kümmel, " Mythische Rede und Heilsgeschehen im Neuen Testament," in *Coniectanea Neotestamentica* (Lund, 1947), XI, p. 124.

14. Bultmann would answer that the Lordship of Christ began with the Easter faith, the understanding of the meaning of the crucifixion, and that he does not give this up.

15. Cf. Chapter VIII on " Eschatology."

16. Kümmel, *loc. cit.,* p. 125.

17. This suggestion will be discussed in Part Three.

18. Karl Barth, *Die kirchliche Dogmatik* (A. G. Zollikon, Zürich, 1948), Vol. III, Pt. 2, pp. 531–537.

19. *Ibid.,* pp. 533 f. Cf. also Part Three.

20. *Ibid.*, p. 534. Cf. also Part Three, where the limitations of Bultmann's existential interpretation are discussed.

21. *Ibid.*, p. 535.

22. *Ibid.*, p. 536.

23. Bultmann, " Neues Testament und Mythologie," p. 53. Cf. also " Zu J. Schniewinds Thesen," p. 152.

24. K. Barth, *op. cit.*, p. 536.

25. For reference to Bultmann as a " rationalist," see Amos Wilder, " Mythology and the New Testament," in the *Journal of Biblical Literature,* Vol. LXIX, II (June, 1950), p. 125.

26. K. Barth, *op. cit.*, p. 536.

27. Arnold J. Toynbee, *A Study of History* (Abridgment of Vols. I–VI by D. C. Somervell; Oxford University Press, 1947), p. 44.

28. Even such a list would be, as we have suggested, an interpretation of the past revealed by the fact that the historian has considered these particular events as of primary importance.

29. Cf. Paul Tillich, *Systematic Theology* (University of Chicago Press, 1951), Vol. I, p. 118: " There is no reality, thing, or event which cannot become a bearer of the mystery of being and enter into a revelatory correlation."

30. This distinction corresponds closely to Bultmann's distinction between *historisch* and *geschichtlich* — *historisch* referring to " neutral " history, and *geschichtlich* to " personal " history, involving decision. Cf. " Neues Testament und Mythologie," p. 47; and Schniewind, " Antwort an Rudolf Bultmann," pp. 117 f.

31. Historical, in the sense of demonstrable.

32. Cf. Col. 2:1, where the meaning is " to see," literally; and Col. 2:18, where both the meaning of the word and the text in general are uncertain.

33. See *horaō* in Arndt and Gingrich, *A Greek-English Lexicon of the New Testament* (University of Chicago Press, 1957); and in Moulton and Milligan, *The Vocabulary of the Greek New Testament* (Hodder and Stoughton, London), 1914–1929.

34. Cf. John Knox, *Chapters in a Life of Paul* (Abingdon Press, 1950), p. 65: " Thus A.D. 35 is a more probable date for

Paul's conversion than any earlier year." Knox apparently dates the crucifixion in A.D. 30.

35. Frederick C. Grant, *An Introduction to New Testament Thought* (Abingdon Press, 1950), p. 227.

36. Kirsopp Lake, "The Ascension," in *The Beginnings of Christianity*, ed. by F. J. Foakes Jackson and Kirsopp Lake (The Macmillan Company, 1933), Vol. V, p. 17.

37. Knox, *op. cit.*, p. 122.

38. *Ibid.*, p. 121.

39. *Ibid.*

40. *Ibid.*, p. 122.

41. Grant, *op. cit.*, p. 227.

42. Bultmann, "Neues Testament und Mythologie," pp. 48 f.; and "Karl Barth, 'Die Auferstehung der Toten,'" pp. 38–64.

43. Cf. Frederick C. Grant, *The Gospels, Their Origin and Their Growth* (Harper & Brothers, 1957), who thinks it is probable that Luke "issued his Gospel about 80 or 85" (p. 127), and that Matthew was written "sometime about the turn of the century, or a little later" (p. 139).

44. If Mark believed that the story of the empty tomb was late, did he also believe that the resurrection story was late? According to his Gospel (excluding ch. 16:9–20) the only reason offered for believing that Jesus had been raised (except for a promise in ch. 16:7) is that the tomb was empty. Presumably, therefore, a report by the women that Jesus had been raised would have included a report of the empty tomb. Cf. John 20:26.

45. In John 20:26 Jesus is still present, in a raised form, "eight days later."

46. Cf. Lake, *loc. cit.*, pp. 18–20.

47. This is generally conceded. Cf. Grant, *An Introduction to New Testament Thought*, p. 227; and Knox, *op. cit.*, p. 120, to cite two recent books.

48. The exceptions to this statement have already been noted in those cases where the resurrection was concretized and historicized. On those occasions the body is misidentified (as in Luke 24:16, 36 ff.) or there are doubts about it (as in John 20:24 ff.; Matt. 28:17).

49. The Book of Hebrews represents a development in the kerygma quite different from that in the Gospels. In Hebrews, Jesus' resurrection is not even mentioned. The emphasis is on his exaltation in glory, not on a resuscitation of the body. Cf. Grant, *An Introduction to New Testament Thought*, pp. 228 f.

CHAPTER VI

1. Bultmann, "Neues Testament und Mythologie," p. 23, n. 2.

2. Max Müller, *The Science of Language* (Charles Scribner's Sons, 1891), Vol. II, p. 456.

3. *Ibid.*, p. 647.

4. George W. Cox, *An Introduction to the Science of Mythology and Folklore* (C. Kegan Paul & Co., London, 1881), p. v.

5. *Ibid.*, p. 13.

6. *Ibid.*, p. 10, n. 1.

7. *Ibid.*, p. 12.

8. *Ibid.*, p. 359.

9. *Ibid.*, p. 360.

10. *Ibid.*, p. 361.

11. Cf. Müller, *op. cit.*, p. 456.

12. *Ibid.*, p. 647.

13. *Ibid.*, pp. 458 f.

14. *Ibid.*, p. 497, n. 1.

15. Bultmann, "Neues Testament und Mythologie," p. 52.

16. *Ibid.*, p. 53.

17. Gustav Stählin, art. "*mythos*," in *Theologisches Wörterbuch zum Neuen Testament*, ed. by Gerhard Kittel (W. Kohlhammer, Stuttgart, 1942), Vol. IV, p. 800.

18. *Ibid.*, p. 799.

19. Hermann Sasse, "Flucht vor dem Dogma," in *Luthertum* (1942), p. 172.

20. Kümmel, "Mythische Rede und Heilsgeschehen im Neuen Testament," pp. 109–131.

21. Martin Dibelius, *Die Formgeschichte des Evangeliums* (2d ed.; J. C. B. Mohr, Tübingen, 1933), p. 265.

22. Ernst Lohmeyer, "Die rechte Interpretation des My-

thologischen," in *Kerygma und Mythos,* p. 155.

23. *Ibid.,* p. 157.

24. *Ibid.*

25. Lynn White, Jr., "Christian Myth and Christian History," in the *Journal of the History of Ideas,* Vol. III, No. 2 (April, 1942), p. 148.

26. Emil Brunner, *The Mediator* (The Westminster Press, 1947), p. 379, n. 1.

27. F. W. J. von Schelling, *Einleitung in die Philosophie der Mythologie* in *Sämmtliche Werke,* Vol. I, Sec. 2.

28. Brunner, *op. cit.,* p. 384.

29. *Ibid.*

30. W. M. Urban, *Language and Reality* (The Macmillan Company, 1939), p. 588.

31. Brunner, *op. cit.,* p. 378, n. 1.

32. Cf. Nathan A. Scott, Jr., "Poetry, Religion, and the Modern Mind," in *The Journal of Religion,* XXXIII, No. 3 (July, 1953), pp. 182–197; and "Poetry and the Crisis of Metaphysics," in *The Christian Scholar,* XXXVI, No. 4 (December, 1953), pp. 273–280. These articles contain excellent discussions of the contemporary problem.

33. For a different understanding of the New Testament's view of history, cf. Oscar Cullmann, *Christ and Time* (The Westminster Press, 1950). Cullmann believes that the New Testament conceives of history as divided into three periods: (a) the period before Creation; (b) the period between Creation and the Parousia; (c) the period after the Parousia which continues indefinitely in time.

34. Ernst Cassirer, *Language and Myth* (Harper & Brothers, 1948), p. 8.

35. *Ibid.,* p. 36.

36. *Ibid.*

37. Lynn White, *loc. cit.,* p. 155.

38. *Ibid.,* pp. 155 f.

39. Cf. John 1:1-3; Col. 1:15-20; Heb. 1:1-4; Rev. 21:6.

40. Reinhold Niebuhr, "The Truth in Myths," in *The Nature of Religious Experience,* ed. by J. S. Bixler, R. L. Calhoun, H. R. Niebuhr (Harper & Brothers, 1937), pp. 119 f.

41. Richard Kroner, "Reason, Reality, Imagination," in

Science, Philosophy and Religion (Conference on Science, Philosophy and Religion in Their Relation to the Democratic Way of Life, Inc., 1943), Third Symposium, p. 42.

42. Cf. Reinhold Niebuhr, *loc. cit.,* p. 133: " Great myths have actually been born out of profound experience."

43. Sallustius, *Concerning the Gods and the Universe,* ed. by A. D. Nock (Cambridge University Press, 1926), p. 9.

44. Karl Storck, *Mozart, sein Leben und Schaffen* (Greiner & Pfeiffer, Stuttgart, 1908), p. 18.

45. Cf. J. J. Bachofen, *Der Mythos von Orient und Okzident* (Manfred Schroeter, Munich, 1926). Thielicke quotes the following passage from this work in " Die Frage der Entmythologisierung des Neuen Testaments," p. 196: " Only the symbol can combine various notions into one unified, total impression. Language connects separate items in succession and presents them to one's mind piecemeal; but in order to be grasped, they should be presented to the soul at a *single* glance." This the symbol (i.e., myth) does.

46. Lynn White, *loc. cit.,* p. 149.

47. Cassirer, *op. cit.,* p. 56.

48. *Ibid.,* p. 58.

49. Urban, *op. cit.,* p. 449.

50. Reinhold Niebuhr, *loc. cit.,* p. 129.

51. Nicolas Berdyaev, *Freedom and the Spirit* (Charles Scribner's Sons, 1935), p. 70.

52. Urban, *op. cit.,* p. 450.

53. Kroner, *loc. cit.,* p. 43.

54. Richard Kroner, " On the Religious Imagination," in *Perspectives on a Troubled Decade: Science, Philosophy and Religion, 1939–1949* (Conference on Science, Philosophy and Religion in Their Relation to the Democratic Way of Life, Inc., 1950), p. 607.

55. Richard Kroner, *The Primacy of Faith* (The Macmillan Company, 1943), p. 163.

56. *Ibid.,* p. 138.

57. William Wordsworth, " Ode: Intimations of Immortality from Recollections of Early Childhood."

58. Cf. Gabriel Marcel, *Être et Avoir* (Fernand Aubier, Paris, 1935), p. 118; and *The Mystery of Being,* Vol. I: *Reflec-*

tion and Mystery (Henry Regnery Company, 1950), pp. 46–48.

59. James Collins, *The Existentialists* (Henry Regnery Company, 1952), p. 221.

60. Reinhold Niebuhr, *loc. cit.*, p. 135.

61. *Ibid.*, p. 120.

62. *Ibid.*, p. 121.

63. Urban, *op. cit.*, p. 587.

64. Berdyaev, *op. cit.*, p. 70.

65. Milton C. Nahm, "Art as One of the Bridges of Cultural Understanding — Retrospect and Prospect," *Perspectives on a Troubled Decade: Science, Philosophy and Religion, 1939–1940*, p. 764.

66. *Urban,* op. cit., p. 591.

67. Reinhold Niebuhr, *loc. cit.*, p. 129.

68. *Ibid.*, p. 130.

69. Walther Eichrodt, *Theologie des Alten Testaments* (2d ed.; Evangelische Verlagsanstalt, Berlin, 1948), II, 3.

70. Paul Tillich, "Mythus, begrifflich und religionspsychologisch," *Die Religion in Geschichte und Gegenwart,* ed. by Gunkel and Zscharnack (J. C. B. Mohr, Tübingen, 1930), Vol. IV, p. 365.

71. Bultmann, *Jesus Christ and Mythology* (Charles Scribner's Sons, 1958), p. 53.

72. Kümmel, *loc. cit.*, pp. 127 ff.

73. Oscar Cullmann, *Königsherrschaft Christi und Kirche im Neuen Testament,* No. 10 of *Theologische Studien,* ed. by Karl Barth (3d ed.; A. G. Zollikon, Zürich, 1950), pp. 14 f. (Eng. tr. "The Kingship of Christ and the Church in the New Testament," in *The Early Church* [The Westminster Press, 1956], pp. 112 f.)

74. Cf. B. J. Kidd, *A History of the Church to A.D. 461* (The Clarendon Press, Oxford, 1922), Vol. I, pp. 219 f.; *Documents Illustrative of the Continental Reformation* (The Clarendon Press, Oxford, 1911), No. 55, pp. 104–106. Also cf. Charles Beard, *The Reformation* (Williams and Norgate, London, 1883), pp. 127 ff.

75. Irenaeus, *Adv. Haer.*, I. 27. 2. Cf. IV. 8. 1.

CHAPTER VII

1. Cf. Francis W. Beare, *The First Epistle of Peter* (The Macmillan Company, 1947), pp. 146, 156.

2. Cf. Bultmann, *Theologie des Neuen Testaments* (J. C. B. Mohr, Tübingen, 1948), I Lieferung, pp. 174–176. (Eng. tr. *Theology of the New Testament*, Vol. I, pp. 175 f.; Charles Scribner's Sons, 1951.) Cf. also W. L. Knox, *St. Paul and the Church of the Gentiles* (Cambridge University Press, 1939), p. 195; and T. K. Abbott, *The Epistles to the Ephesians and to the Colossians* (Charles Scribner's Sons, 1909), p. 115.

3. Ignatius, *Ep. to the Phil.*, IX.

4. Cf. p. 89.

5. Bultmann, *Das Evangelium des Johannes* (Vandenhoeck & Ruprecht, Göttingen, 1950), p. 477.

6. C. H. Dodd, *The Interpretation of the Fourth Gospel* (Cambridge University Press, 1953), p. 395.

CHAPTER VIII

1. Bultmann, " Neues Testament und Mythologie," p. 46.

2. *Ibid.*

3. *Ibid.*, p. 49.

4. *Ibid.*

5. *Ibid.*, p. 51. Cf. II Cor. 6:2.

6. *Ibid.* Cf. II Cor. 4:12.

7. *Ibid.*, p. 52.

8. Cf. H. D. Wendland, *Die Mitte der paulinischen Botschaft* (Vanderhoeck & Ruprecht, Göttingen, 1935).

9. Kümmel, *loc. cit.*, p. 122. Cf. also: Kümmel, *Die Eschatologie der Evangelien* (1936), pp. 21 ff.; Hans Pribnow, *Die johanneische Anschauung vom "Leben"* (University of Greifswald, 1934), pp. 102 ff.; Gustav Stählin, " Zum Problem der johanneischen Eschatologie," *Zeitschrift für die neutestamentliche Wissenschaft*, Vol. XXXIII (1934), pp. 225 ff.; Ph. H. Menoud, " L'originalité de la Pensée johannique," *Revue de théologie et de philosophie*, Nouvelle série, Vol. XXVIII (1940), pp. 245 ff.

10. Althaus, *op. cit.*, Vol. II, p. 473.

11. *Ibid.*, p. 493.

12. *Ibid.*, pp. 495–498.

13. *Ibid.*, p. 499.

14. *Ibid.*, p. 500.

15. *Ibid.*, p. 504.

16. *Ibid.*

17. Schniewind, *loc. cit.*, pp. 123 ff.

18. Leopold von Ranke, *Über die Epochen der neueren Geschichte* (8th ed.; Duncker, Munich, 1921).

19. Paul Tillich, "The Kingdom of God and History," in *The Kingdom of God and History* (Willet, Clark & Company, 1938), p. 113.

20. Tillich, *The Kingdom of God and History*, p. 127.

21. *Ibid.*

22. *Ibid.*

23. Nicolas Berdyaev, *The Destiny of Man* (The Centenary Press, London, 1937), Part III. Also *The Meaning of History, passim* (Geoffrey Bles, London, reprinted in 1949).

24. Berdyaev, *The Destiny of Man*, p. 368.

25. *Ibid.*

26. Berdyaev, *The Meaning of History*, p. 204.

27. Cf. Reinhold Niebuhr, *Beyond Tragedy* (Charles Scribner's Sons, 1936); *The Nature and Destiny of Man* (Charles Scribner's Sons, 1945), Vol. II, Ch. 10; *Faith and History* (Charles Scribner's Sons, 1949).

28. Reinhold Niebuhr, *The Nature and Destiny of Man*, Vol. II, p. 299.

29. *Ibid.*, p. 301.

30. *Ibid.*, pp. 290 f.

31. Niebuhr, *Beyond Tragedy*, p. 22.

32. *Ibid.*, p. 24.

33. Augustine, *De Civitate Dei*, Bk. 15, Ch. 1.

CHAPTER IX

1. Mark 10:15 and parallels. This verse, in the light of v. 14, should be understood as referring to the present, as well as to the future. On the verse, see Vincent Taylor, *The Gospel According to St. Mark* (Macmillan & Co., Ltd., London, 1953), p. 423: "The implication is not far distant that in a true sense Jesus himself is the Kingdom; to use the word of Origen,

Comm. Mt. t. xiv. 7, He is *autobasileia.*"

2. Joel 2:28 ff. (Heb. 3:1 ff.) ; Ezek. 36:27; 37:14; Isa. 44:3; Zech. 12:10; Num. 11:29 (interpreted eschatologically in Midrash on Ps. 14:7). Cf. Strack and Billerbeck, *Kommentar zum Neuen Testament* (C. H. Becksche, Munich, 1924), Vol. II, p. 134.

3. I Enoch 49:3; Pss. of Sol. 17:42; Test. of Levi 18:6–7; Test. of Judah 24:2–3. Cf. Zadokite Fragments 2:10 (perhaps 2d century B.C.).

4. Bultmann, *Die Geschichte der synoptischen Tradition* (3d ed.; Vandenhoeck & Ruprecht, Göttingen, 1957), pp. 263 f.

5. C. G. Montefiore, *The Synoptic Gospels* (2d ed.; Macmillan and Co., Ltd., London, 1927), Vol. I, p. 20.

6. Wrede's view of the Messianic secret must be maintained. It was his analysis of its development that was, I believe, in error.

7. Cf. W. O. E. Oesterley, *The Jews and Judaism During the Greek Period* (Society for Promoting Christian Knowledge, London, 1941), pp. 278–289, for a brief discussion of demonology in the Old Testament, in Persian religion, and in post-Biblical Jewish literature. No exorcisms are mentioned.

8. Strack and Billerbeck, *op. cit.,* Vol. IV, pp. 501–535. Cf. W. O. E. Oesterley, " The Belief in Angels and Demons," in *Judaism and Christianity,* Vol. I: *The Age of Transition,* ed. by Oesterley (The Macmillan Company, 1937), pp. 200–209.

9. Israel Abrahams, *Studies in Pharisaism and the Gospels,* First Series (Cambridge University Press, 1917), pp. 110 f.

10. S. Vernon McCasland, *By the Finger of God* (The Macmillan Company, 1951), p. 79. Cf. pp. 78–80.

11. Note the plural " *exorcists* who used a lyre," but only David is referred to.

12. The Book of Jubilees 10:10–14.

13. *Antiquities of the Jews,* VIII. II. 5.

14. McCasland, *op. cit.,* p. 69.

15. *Ibid.,* p. 66. Cf. Adolf Deissmann, *Light from the Ancient East* (4th ed.; Harper & Brothers, 1922), pp. 135 f., 256, 259–281, 307 f. Also Albrecht Dieterich, *Eine Mithrasliturgie* (2d ed.; B. G. Teubner, Leipzig, 1910).

16. Cf. McCasland, *op. cit.*, pp. 92 ff., who also believes that Jesus' exorcisms were Messianic in character, and were considered so not only by the early church but also by Jesus himself, and by the possessed whom he exorcised.

17. C. K. Barrett, *The Holy Spirit and the Gospel Tradition* (Society for Promoting Christian Knowledge, London, 1947), p. 62.

18. Cf. Barrett, *op. cit.*, p. 67, who refers to the quoted Biblical passages. I am completely in agreement with Barrett here, and very much in his debt.

19. Cf. John 14:16 ff., and C. H. Dodd, *op. cit.*, p. 395.

20. Cf. Bultmann, *Theology of the New Testament*, Vol. I; Oscar Cullmann, *Christ and Time;* C. H. Dodd, *The Parables of the Kingdom;* Joachim Jeremias, *The Parables of Jesus;* W. G. Kümmel, *Promise and Fulfillment;* T. W. Manson, *The Teaching of Jesus;* William Manson, *Jesus the Messiah;* Rudolf Otto, *The Kingdom of God and the Son of Man;* etc.

21. In this parable, Matt. 25:30; and in chs. 8:12 and 22:13.

22. For other examples of the same phenomenon, cf. Joachim Jeremias, *The Parables of Jesus* (S.C.M. Press Ltd., London, 1955).

23. Cf. I. Enoch 41:9; 51:1–2; 55:3–4; 61:8; 62:2–3; 69:26–29. It is possible, however, that these passages are Christian in origin.

24. Bultmann, " Neues Testament und Mythologie," p. 34.

25. John 6:39, 40, 44, 54; 8:24; 12:48; 13:36; 14:2 f. Cf. I John 2:18, 28; 3:2–3; 4:17.

26. Bultmann, *Das Evangelium des Johannes, passim;* and *Theology of the New Testament*, Vol. II, pp. 3–92 *passim*.

27. Matt. 13:44. Cf. Matt. 11:25 and Luke 10:21; Eph. 3:9; Col. 1:26; 2:2 f.; II Cor. 4:3; Luke 19:42.

28. Acts 3:7, etc. Cf. Rom. 1:4, where Paul associates the manifestation of power with the resurrection. In this case, Jesus was designated Son of God in power by the resurrection.

CHAPTER X

1. Karl Barth, *Die kirchliche Dogmatik*, Vol. III, Pt. 2, p. 534.

2. Bultmann, " Neues Testament und Mythologie," p. 44.

3. *Ibid.,* pp. 24, 44.

4. This is shown by the fact that the virgin birth is never referred to in the gospel narrative after it has once been recorded. It is a late addition to the kerygma, not known by Paul or Mark.

5. See, for example, René Laurentin, *Structure et Théologie de Luc I–II* (J. Gabalda et Cie., Paris, 1957). There are almost two hundred pages of text on Luke, chs. 1 and 2, followed by a bibliography of five hundred titles.

6. Cf. Mishnah, *Ketuboth* 5. 2.

7. The pre-existence of the Messiah is a belief reflected in Jewish literature. Cf. I Enoch 48:2, 3, 6; 62:7; IV Ezra 7:28; 12:32; 13:26, 52; 14:9; Sibylline Oracles V. 414.

CHAPTER XI

1. Bultmann, " Neues Testament und Mythologie," p. 47.

2. James Collins, *The Existentialists* (Henry Regnery Company, 1952), p. 138.

3. Cf. Emil Brunner, *Christianity and Civilization,* First Part (Charles Scribner's Sons, 1948), p. 132: " The maximum of dependence on God is the maximum of (man's) freedom, and . . . any attempt to get out of the dependence on God leads to slavery." Cf. also Brunner's *Man in Revolt* (The Westminster Press, 1947), pp. 262 f.

4. Bultmann, " Neues Testament und Mythologie," p. 47.

5. Bultmann, " Zu J. Schniewinds Thesen," p. 141.

6. Cf. William Manson, *Jesus the Messiah* (The Westminster Press, 1946), p. 172: " For the evidence of a more inward appreciation of the meaning of the Messiah's death on the part of the primitive church we have . . . to look away from Acts to St. Paul."

7. Cf. John Knox, *Chapters in a Life of Paul,* pp. 133 f., 151 f.

8. Vincent Taylor, *The Atonement in New Testament Teaching* (2d ed.; The Epworth Press, London, 1950), p. 120. See also p. 121 for references.

9. It must be added, however, that even in the days of the Temple, Judaism required repentance along with sacrifice if

sins were to be forgiven. On this whole subject, see George Foot Moore, *Judaism,* Vol. I, pp. 497–606; J. Bonsirven, *Le Judaïsme Palestinien,* Vol. II, pp. 92–105; A. B. Davidson, *Theology of the Old Testament,* pp. 306–356; A. Büchler, *Studies in Sin and Atonement in the Rabbinic Literature of the First Century;* F. C. N. Hicks, *The Fullness of Sacrifice;* W. O. E. Oesterley, *Sacrifice in Ancient Israel;* Johs. Pedersen, *Israel,* Vol. III–IV, pp. 299–375.

10. Cf. Royden Keith Yerkes, *Sacrifice in Greek and Roman Religions and Early Judaism* (Charles Scribner's Sons, 1952), p. 135.

11. There is, of course, also an important relation between the Lord's Supper in the church and the eating of the sacrifices in Israel.

12. Cf. Pedersen, *Israel,* Vol. III–IV, pp. 300 ff., and *passim.*

13. Cf. Ex. 22:29; II Kings 16:3; 17:17; 21:6; Jer. 7:31; 32:35; Ezek. 16:20; 23:37 ff.

14. Pedersen, *op. cit.,* p. 366. In his commentary on Lev. 1:4, Alfred Bertholet interprets the laying of the hand on the victim's head in the same way. Also Yerkes, *Sacrifice in Greek and Roman Religions and Early Judaism,* p. 134.

15. Pedersen, *op. cit.,* p. 373.

16. James Denney, *The Death of Christ* (3d ed.; Hodder and Stoughton, London, 1903), p. 177.

17. Isaac Watts' hymn "When I Survey the Wondrous Cross."

18. Bultmann, "Neues Testament und Mythologie," p. 46.

19. *Ibid.,* p. 48.

CHAPTER XII

1. Bultmann, "Neues Testament und Mythologie," pp. 47 f.

2. *Ibid.,* p. 50.

3. *Ibid.,* p. 49.

4. *Ibid.*

5. *Ibid.*

6. *Ibid.,* pp. 47 f.

7. *Ibid.,* p. 48.

8. *Ibid.*

9. *Ibid.,* p. 33.

10. *Ibid.*

CHAPTER XIII

1. George Foot Moore, *Judaism* (Harvard University Press, 1944), Vol. I, p. 239.

2. Brooke Foss Westcott, *A General Survey of the History of the Canon of the New Testament* (7th ed.; Macmillan & Co., Ltd., London, 1896), p. 12.

3. *Ibid.,* pp. 343 f.

4. *Ibid.,* p. 356.

5. *Ibid.,* pp. 402 f.

6. *Ibid.,* p. 450. Quoted from Luther's *Werke,* ed. by Walch. Vol. XIV, p. 150.

7. This is not intended to imply that God's Word is not and never has been communicated by any medium other than the Bible. We cannot deny revelation outside of Scripture, and we cannot any longer make the clear-cut distinctions in the Hellenistic period between " Greek " and " Hebraic " thought that have been made in the past. What is intended in this statement is that the Word of God as recorded in the Bible must be normative in the church for all saving knowledge communicated outside of the church.

8. *The Interpretation of the Bible,* ed. by C. W. Dugmore (Society for Promoting Christian Knowledge, London, 1944), p. 72.

INDEX

SUBJECTS

SCRIPTURE REFERENCES